the ultimate low point® cooking, ingredient and recipe guide

THE GUILT FREE GOURMET

2019 Cooking Guide

Follow us online at:
The Web: www.theguiltfreegourmet.net
Connect: @dhallakx7
Facebook: The Guilt Free Gourmet
Instagram: TheGuiltFreeGourmet
Twitter: @GLTFreeGourmet

Copyright©2018 by Daniel Hallak
Book design by Daniel Hallak
Edited by Peggy Barr & Mary Geiler
Photographs by Daniel Hallak & various Royalty Free Image Galleries
The Guilt Free Gourmet is a division of The Low Point Gourmet LLC.
The Guilt Free Gourmet Low Point Cooking Guide, 1st Edition 2019
The Author grants permission to reprint this publication **for personal use only**

Kitchen
CONVERSION CHART
CUPS & SPOONS

TSP	TBSP	FL OZ	CUP	PINT	QUART	GALLON
3	1	1/2	1/16	1/32	–	–
6	2	1	1/8	1/16	1/32	–
12	4	2	1/4	1/8	1/16	–
18	6	3	3/8	–	–	–
24	8	4	1/2	1/4	1/8	1/32
36	12	6	3/4	–	–	–
48	16	8	1	1/2	1/4	1/16
–	64	32	4	2	1	1/4
–	256	128	16	8	4	1

NOTE:

These recipes were developed over the course of many months. WW periodically adjusts the point values of certain ingredients in their database. As a result, there may be a 1 point difference between what my recipes were when they were developed, versus what their point values are "now". You are all encouraged to enter these recipes into your app, to double check the current accuracy of their points at this present date.

LEGAL DISCLAIMERS:

The Guilt Free Gourmet® 2018

Though we have copyright protection over this publication and the materials here-in, we at The Guilt Free Gourmet want to make sure you understand that **you have our full and complete permission to have this material printed for your private use**! **If you are a home cook or a cooking enthusiast, please know that we wish for you to be able to print this material, either at home, or at a business that offers printing services, such as Staples, Office Depot, Kinkos, etc.**

If you try to take this to a printing center and they say that they can't print it, PLEASE tell them to look at the disclaimer cited above. The Author has expressly stated that he (me) has given permission for you to print it... Then poke him/her in the chest to establish dominance. Howling loudly while pointing at their copy machine.

Weight Watchers International & WW®

The Guilt Free Gourmet is not affiliated with, nor is it endorsed by Weight Watchers International, Inc. (now WW®). Weight Watchers has not reviewed this publication for accuracy or suitability for WW members.

Weight Watchers, WW®, Point, Points, Smart Points, SP's and Freestyle are all registered trademarks of Weight Watchers International, Inc. Authentic information about the program is only available at your local WW workshop or online through the WW website and mobile app. The information and recipes contained within this guide are based solely on the recollections and assumptions of The Guilt Free Gourmet. The information and recipes are not warranted for any purpose by the author other than for educational purposes and for reference under fair use doctrine.

All readers are encouraged to go to a WW Workshop or the WW website for actual WW information and to also enter the listed ingredients of my recipes themselves into the Recipe Builder. Point values for certain ingredients change and are updated periodically by WW®, which may change the point values we are suggesting to be accurate for our recipes at this time.

This guide is in **NO WAY** meant to be a replacement for the WW Program. It is merely developed and intended for use as an educational cooking guide to complement the instructional materials and resources provided by WW to its members.

Any non-generic recipes within this guide were developed by me. All Point values were determined by entering the ingredients, measurements and servings into the Recipe Builder within the WW mobile App that is only available to paying members of the system. I strongly encourage anyone interested in developing a healthier lifestyle to join and follow the strategies for healthy living provided by Weight Watchers International (WW®).

All use of the terms Weight Watchers, WW, Point, Points, Smart Points, SP's and Freestyle in the following guide are used SOLELY for reference purposes, as is appropriate and allowed under fair use doctrine.

This publication is dedicated to my loving wife, whom I will never deserve. You have stood by me, a steadfast rock, weathering every storm and tempest that we've faced. You have supported and encouraged me during every phase of the past 18 years, and have held my hand through the darkest nights. Thank you for saying "Yes" all those years ago and for putting up with me ever since. On a positive, at least there's a whole lot less of me for you to put up with now.

- Daniel

Contents

2019 | *Cooking Guide - First Edition*

0sp Cheesy Broccoli Stuffed Chicken with Mashed Cauliflower.

2sp Cocoa Banana Peanut Butter Short Stack

Opening Thoughts

Back in December 2017, I joined Weight Watchers. I started my journey in search of weight loss. Never in a million years, would have imagined that a year later, I'd be sitting here, click-clacking away at my dinosaur of a laptop, writing a cookbook. I also never would have thought of where that decision would take me. I never would have imagined, just by joining Weight Watchers, I would have the opportunity to someday be able to help and offer encouragement and support to so many people, simply by cooking dinner for my wife and kids. Now, a year later, I find myself sitting here, click-clacking way on my Laptopasaurus, writing a cookbook. This is all because of you folks in Connect. You all pushed me to do this, you all kept jabbering away at me to make this guide, so here'ya go. Merry Christmas... Seriously, talk about perfect timing!

Most everything in this guide is a direct request from one person or another in Connect. That delicious looking **4sp** Beef Stroganoff that's on the cover? It was made for **@andmatsmom** after she posted in Connect about the loss of her son and asked if I could make a low point version of his favorite dish for her. The tutorial for low point pasta? It came from seeing people constantly talking about how much they missed eating REAL pasta, due to the high points cost. Every one of the 30 sauces in the Sauce Section was specifically requested by people in Connect. The Recipe Builder tutorial came from recognizing the need for it, when night after night, people talked about how much they missed having food they loved pre-program. I can't even begin to describe to you, how amazing the feeling is, knowing that you're helping people who had been struggling. Then later on being tagged in their posts showing how they are reworking recipes, making low point tamales from scratch, baking low point desserts... and that they feel in control now. It's AWESOME!!!

Getting to this point has been a 6 month labor of love. I was originally planning to compile every single recipe I had ever posted and have a gigantic cookbook. After 3 months, I realized I was cramming so much information into this first section alone, that it actually was an amazing cooking guide by itself. The response this guide has received has been so completely unexpected. I can't believe how many people have said it's been life changing for them. As of the date of this publication it's been download over 47,000 times! In only 3.5 months!

I want you to finish reading through this cooking guide and feel empowered in your kitchen. I want you to try out new techniques and ingredients that you wouldn't have before. I want you to close this baby, open up the Recipe Builder and start playing around with modifying recipes, like a rockstar. Between the low point Foundation recipes and the low point sauce recipes, you should be able to look at almost ANY recipe, from any website or magazine, then start dropping points like Chuck Norris drops baddies by punching them with his beard. Now... let's get to it!

Note: How To Read Measurements In This Guide

There has been some confusion on Connect from some folks about how to read the way that I write my measurements. So here goes:

1-1/4 = 1 and 1/4 of something, as in 1 and 1/4 teaspoons
2-1/2 = 2 and 1/2 of something, as in 2 and 1/2 teaspoons
3-3/4 = 3 and 3/4 of something, as in 3 and 3/4 teaspoons

Introduction

"... if I would have known all of those years ago that I could lose weight without any exercise, and without having to eat twigs and rabbit food, I could have saved myself a good 2 decades of being miserable..."

Hi there, my name is Daniel, but most of you know me from Connect as dhallakx7. As of the writing of this cookbook, I'm a 41-year-old stay at home dad to my 2 special needs toddlers, Rachel (Autism) and Jesse (Down Syndrome). Prior to this, I worked as a Graphic Designer & Web Developer for a really great company. I had just received a big promotion, but once Jesse was born preemie and his diagnosis was finally confirmed, our priorities had to change. I became Mr. Mom.

I still remember the night in 3rd grade when I turned from liking food, to wanting to gorge on food. My best friend Bart and I went to a high school soccer game with my older brother. At that game I saw something that I'd never seen before. A food vendor showed up in the bleachers pushing a food cart. He was using it to make hot, sugar coated mini cake donuts, fresh to order. I remember running down to that cart with my friend, looking at the fresh donuts, then immediately running up to my brother and asking for the money to buy some... then to buy some more... then to buy some more. And that's where it started.

I spent the better part of the next 30 years going from "husky" to overweight, eventually becoming heavy enough to be classified as obese. I only went swimming 3 or 4 times in the past 25 years out of shame for how I looked. I would make excuses not to see friends who were visiting from out of town, whom I hadn't seen in years. Heck, I wouldn't even change in the same room as my wife because I was

The new and improved Dad model 2.0, now available with dual child restraints, improved mileage and an extended warranty

Nov. '17   Oct. '18

embarrassed about my body. Yet, did it make me want to change and lose weight? Nope, I figured it wasn't worth it.

In order to lose weight, I was going to be eating nothing but rice cakes and tasteless diet food. I would have to start going to the gym, running and stop eating all the foods that I loved to eat. People on diets are always so miserable and complain about what they can't eat, how their diet de jour doesn't allow them to have sugar, or they are cutting all carbs, or they are doing "cleanses" or whatever insane dietary deprivation is the current trend. Why in the heck would I want to do that? I'd rather be fat and eating than be skinny and surviving on rice cakes, bean curd and sadness. But, when I finally hit my mental rock bottom, I stumbled upon an article online late at night. It was written by a female blogger who tried Weight Watchers for one month without doing any exercise and without giving up eating regular food. She ended up losing 5 pounds over the course of the month without working out, while still eating normal foods and staying within her Weight Watchers daily allotment of "Smart Points". I figured it was worth a shot as I had no

Don't let food manipulate you, learn to manipulate your food

Use The Recipe Builder

- Lower the fat, calories, sugar, and carbs of foods by swapping ingredients
- Get MORE points to spend elsewhere in your day by making meals as low in points as possible
- Retrain your brain to automatically think of ingredient substitutions, making this journey livable, sustainable, and enjoyable with GREAT food

Cont.

Introduction

desire to stop eating normal food and no desire to exercise (at that time).

The first few weeks were difficult but manageable. I was losing weight, I wasn't working out, but dear Lord, there was so much food that I missed eating that I couldn't have because it was so high in points. Then it happened... I found the App's recipe builder and that pretty much changed everything.

I immediately realized the full possibilities the tool offered. I bought a cooking magazine from the grocery store that had a recipe on the cover for a skillet full of baked rolls covered in tons of cheese, marinara sauce, pepperoni and Italian sausage. The type of meal there is NO WAY you could ever eat on Weight Watchers and stay within your points. I input the entire recipe into the recipe builder, along with the suggested servings, and saw that it would be 11 points PER ROLL! And there were 18 rolls in the skillet. I was determined to find a way, with the app, to be able to swap out ingredients and make a low point healthier version that I could have.

I scoured Connect for ingredient swap ideas and even came up with a few ideas of my own. I started swapping out regular cheese for fat free cheese and mixed in some plain yogurt for added creaminess. I adjusted spice amounts, checked how much wine I could cut with water to reduce the points and still taste it in a sauce. I tried getting as creative as

I possibly could to make the skillet as low fat and low calorie as possible.

I ended up dropping it from 11sp per serving down to 3sp per serving. That's the moment when I realized that you really CAN eat almost anything on Weight Watchers without being constrained by your daily allowed points. You just need to learn how to make healthier versions of your favorite dishes.

My "WHY" (for this book)

I was an online only WW member and a Freestyle Godzilla. I bulldozed through the program and lost 53lbs in 3.5 months while eating food like this every single day, without ANY exercise. But as a result I lacked empathy for other members who I would see struggling in Connect.

A few weeks after reaching goal, I decided to attend my 1 free Weight Watchers meeting at the local office in Santa Clarita, California. It completely changed my life. I went in a cocky guy, unable to understand why anyone would have trouble staying on plan when all they had to do was cook. I couldn't relate. At that meeting I was kicked square in the face by a room full of hurt people, in pain, sharing their struggles and how hard it is for them to not be able to eat the foods they want. The amount and depth of the hurt that I heard in that room from most of the members, while I didn't struggle at all, made me feel as heartbroken as a long-distance runner taking a walk through an amputee ward.

It inspired me to start sharing recipes on Connect with everyone so I could help give hope to those who were losing their battle.

The Fat Free "cheese hack" lets you have melty cheese for an entire pan of Lasagna for only 4sp in total

Ultra Low Point Pie Crust

1sp Potato Flakes Breading

12sp Fresh Pasta

12sp Store-Bought

Swaps, Hacks, & Tips

Low Point Ingredient Substitutions

Retrain Your Brain

If you think about it, the primary purpose of the Recipe Builder in the Weight Watchers App is to make us WANT to cook our food with less fat, calories, sugars and carbs. Every time you lower the point value of a recipe with ingredient swaps, you have cut 1 or all those 4 things.

Subbing Butter Out

Molly McButter Fat Free Sprinkles

This stuff is amazing. It's a fine powder that dissolves perfectly in liquids and gives the flavor and color of butter. You can use up to 1 tablespoon for 0 points. It's a go-to staple in my kitchen for sauces.

I Can't Believe It's Not Butter- Light

Don't get one of the other types of I Can't Believe It's Not Butter spreads. Make sure you get the one that says "Light" and scan it to make sure. It is a butter flavored spread that can be used perfectly in place of butter, but at a fraction of the points. A ¼ cup is only 6sp, while ¼ cup of real butter is 20sp. Perfect for when you MUST use butter, but need to reduce the points, calories, and fat.

ULTRA Low Point Pie Crusts

Kellogg's All-Bran or Fiber One

Traditionally for a pie crust you'd use crushed up graham crackers. But the amount of graham crackers and butter for that is around 36-46sp. If you put All-Bran or Fiber One cereal in a food processor with a little bit of FF Yogurt and some 0 point sweetener (monkfruit, swerve etc) and sugar free maple syrup, along with some Molly Mcbutter or I Can't Believe It's Not Butter, you can make an entire pie crust for only 7sp.

Yogurt For Oil In Cake Mixes

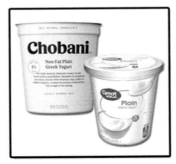

Fat Free Plain Greek Yogurt

Yogurt is a good substitute for mayo and sour cream in most recipes, though it can easily curdle when introduced into sauces or hot liquids. Let the liquids or dishes cool a bit before you bring the yogurts up to temperature and mix them in.

Fat Free Plain Yogurt

I personally prefer to use Plain Yogurt as a substitute for oil rather than Greek Yogurt, as it is thinner and more closely resembles the viscosity of oil.

Subbing with Yogurt and Tofu

Now This One's Interesting

Along with being used to sub for oil in baking, you can also use FF Yogurts to sub for mayo, sour cream, milk and even cream in different applications. Use it instead of cream or milk with mashed cauliflower, and sub it for mayo in dips and dressings after a few tests. Note: If you are allergic to dairy, you can use Tofu in place of yogurt in recipes. Simply blend a bit of medium-firm tofu with a little almond milk. It works like a charm.

SF Maple Syrup Instead of Honey

Sugar Free Maple Syrups

As delicious and complex a flavor as honey is, it is also very high in points and sugars. Sugar free maple syrup is a very viable substitute in most all recipes that call for honey with hardly any of the points. I use it as a sub in most all sauces, glazes and baked goods. The flavor isn't as sweet, but it frees up so many points in a recipe that you then have the luxury to add some sugar if needed and stay well below honey in total points.

Low Point Breading for Meats & Veggies

Mashed Potato Flakes

In a later section of the book I have a recipe for breading that is only 1sp per serving. The recipe is mostly mashed potato flakes, but also has the bare minimum amounts of Panko and Regular bread crumbs to keep those at 0sp. It works amazingly well in either an Air Fryer or a traditional oven.

Melting Fat Free Cheese Hack

Fat Free Mozzarella & Cheddar

This is a game changer. Using this hack you can "cheese" an entire pan of Lasagna with 2 cups (really 3) of melty Mozzarella for only 4sp. The biggest problem with FF cheese is that it doesn't melt. That problem is solved if you mix it with a bit of FF plain (or Greek) yogurt. Sounds wrong, but it's amazing. Mix any amount of Kraft (or other brand) Fat Free shredded cheese with about 3/4 as much FF plain yogurt and mix until it forms a cheesy goopy mixture. Use it on Chicken Parmesan, Lasagnas or stuffed in a chicken breast. It works like a charm.

Fresh Pasta to the Rescue

Don't Give Up Your Pasta!!!!

On the previous page you can see a picture of 12sp of fresh pasta next to 12sp of store bought pasta. If you learn to make it yourself, it's lower in carbs and calories than the store-bought stuff, tastes better and is MUCH easier to proportion. Using fresh Pasta Sheets for an entire pan of lasagna makes the whole thing 700 less calories and removes around 186g of carbs. In this guide, I'll show you how to make your own pasta without any special equipment.

0sp Italian Sausage, Chorizo, & More

with Seasoned Ground Turkey

A quick search of Google will turn up hundreds of recipes for DIY sausages. It doesn't take much work to convert a recipe for making your own PORK Italian sausage to be viable with ground turkey. You just need to modify the seasonings a little bit.   By using the seasoning recipes in this book you'll be able to season ground turkey to be a viable 0sp replacement for chorizo, Italian sausage, breakfast sausage and even ground beef in recipes.

Quickly Ripen Yellow Bananas

Sweeten up those baked goods

Ever tried to make a banana bread or another baked item that calls for "very ripe" bananas, but all that you have are the firm yellow ones without a fleck of black on them? Here's a quick fix. Throw the firm bananas (in their skin) onto a pie pan, and bake them at 325 degrees for 15-20 minutes.

Pudding without Milk or Yogurt

Thickening without Dairy or Fat

It's one of the annoying things about pudding, it just won't thicken if you use water, soy milk, almond milk or whatever. Well, that's not the case. If you use HALF as much of a non fatty fluid as the directions call for milk, it works. If you want it to have the consistency of regular pudding, use 1 cup of COLD liquid in place of the 2 cups milk. If you are wanting it thick enough to where it can keep its shape for a frosting, use 2/3 cup. So, use (1) 1oz packet of instant pudding and 1 cup cold water for pudding or 2/3 cup for frosting.

Jicama is a surprisingly good substitute for french fries

Research Tirelessly

Other than telling you to dig into the Recipe Builder, this is the best advice I can give you on this food journey. When it comes to ideas for food substitutions, the Internet is your friend. Most of the things that I've thought to try came from late night Google searches, trying to figure out how I could substitute or make lower versions of things.

THINK OUTSIDE THE BOX!! I didn't reinvent the wheel with this stuff, I just pulled it from somewhere else and Weight Watcher-ized it. A prime example is the Low Point Pie Crust. I found the idea for that on a Diabetic cooking site because they have to drastically reduce their sugar intake. When I wanted to find Osp potato alternatives for French fries, I figured that I should look on "low carb" cooking forums and sites. The goal of this system is to retrain us to make healthier food choices, and the goal of the recipe builder is to subtlety push us towards making our foods as healthy (and lower in points) as possible.

Challenge yourself to think. Find or try new ways to substitute ingredients. Then you'll be able to have pretty much anything, guilt free, with a little bit of time in the kitchen.

Potato Substitutes

Osp Potato Alternatives

A few months back I got determined to have a big bowl of nacho cheese fries. Only one problem, potatoes are very high in points. I spent days combing through low carb cooking sites and compiled a short list of what people on low carb diets use to sub for potatoes. I then went about trying out the different veggies. The following are listed in no particular order.

Rutabagas

Rutabaga is a root vegetable that falls into the same family as broccoli, brussel sprouts and kale. Once it's washed and peeled, a rutabaga's orange flesh is similar in texture and flavor to a turnip.

Celery Root (listed as "celeriac" in the App)

Celeriac has a mild celery flavor and is often used as a flavoring in soups and stews. It can also be used on its own, usually mashed, or used in casseroles, au gratins and baked dishes. It has a naturally savory flavor.

Jicama

Jicama resembles a large light-brown colored turnip. The white, creamy interior has a very crisp texture somewhat similar to a firm apple or raw potato. Cooking jicama or serving it raw are equally tasty ways to prepare this lightly sweet root

Pureed/Mashed Fruit & Veggies in Cake

More alternatives to oil in baking

As well as using fat free plain yogurt like we mentioned earlier, no sugar added and pureed fruits and vegetables are perfect 1:1 swaps in baking for most, if not all, of the recommended liquid ingredients listed on boxed cake mixes. Make sure to scan labels first though, as some brands DO add sugar.

DIY Self Rising Flour

Perfect for Gluten Free folks

Members with Gluten sensitivities have a rough time with a lot of recipes, especially the 2 ingredient dough that we all know and love. Simply add 1 1/2 teaspoons of baking powder and 1/4 teaspoon of salt to every 1 cup of WHATEVER flour you would like to use. Whether it's gluten free, whole wheat, cornmeal or any type of flour you want.

Simply use that formula and you'll have your own self rising flour.

Replacing Heavy Cream

Thickening soups, sauces, gravies

One of the most annoying things about "normal" recipes is how much heavy cream goes into EVERYTHING. In the Sauces section, I'll be showing you how I use various ingredients to completely eliminate it by using cornstarch, almond milk, fat free plain yogurt, nonfat milk, powdered milk, silken tofu and even instant mashed potato flakes in some instances to act as a thickener in sauces.

Fat Free Cheeses

The Hard To Find Ingredient

One of the hardest to find ingredients for a lot of folks is fat free cheese. You can "cheese" an entire Lasagna with my fat free cheese hack for 4 points versus 19 points for reduced fat. Also, 1 single 8oz packet of fat free cream cheese is only 6 points compared to the 23 points for 1/3 fat cream cheese. I and others in Connect have had the most luck finding fat free cheeses at Wal-Mart.

Cheese Flavored Seasoning Powders

Molly McButter & Kernel Seasons

I use these specifically for when I make my low point cheese sauces. A little bit of these guys goes a LONG way to doc up a cheese sauce. "Kernel Seasons" also sells many different flavored seasonings that are usually found near the popcorn at the grocery store or in the spice aisle. It's saltier though so you'll need to adjust the recipe's salt accordingly.

Make Your Own 0sp Cream Cheese

Seriously... it's simple

Later in this book I'll give you a recipe on how to use MILD flavored fat free plain Greek yogurt to make your own very tasty cream cheese alternative at home for any cream cheese recipe. It completely kicks down the doors to so many different dips, spreads and appetizers. Making it couldn't be any easier.

Flavored Cooking Sprays Instead of Oil

Obvious, but deserves a shout-out

I personally use a TON of butter flavored cooking spray. When seasoning raw meats, I hit both sides with butter flavored or olive oil flavored cooking spray to help flavor the meat. You can also use the butter spray on popcorn. Use the olive oil spray to lightly hit the top of homemade low point hummus or other dishes instead of drizzling olive oil on them. There are tons of ways to use flavored sprays as a seasoning.

Powdered Peanut Butter

Dehydrated and nearly Fat Free PB

Powdered peanut butter, regardless of the brand, is freaking awesome. You can mix it with water to rehydrate it for use as regular peanut butter or you can add the powder to recipes and baked goods to give a PB flavor without all the added mass, points, or stickiness. It's great in everything from smoothies to satay sauces, baking mixes or mixed with pudding or yogurt. The best part being that it's a fraction of the points of regular peanut butter.

0 Point Natural Sweeteners

Natural Sugar Replacements

First things first, just because something isn't normal sugar doesn't mean that it's poison, folks. If you don't like sweeteners, then more power to'ya, but some folks need them for dietary restrictions, and others (like me) don't mind them because... well, points.

I wanted to list just a few of the popular types of natural sweeteners that you can use in place of sugar that are 0 points, starting with my favorites.

* **SWERVE:** Swerve is a brand of sweetener that is derived from Erythritol, which is sugar alcohol. It has zero calories, zero net carbs and is certified non-GMO and non-glycemic. It is a great 1:1 replacement for regular sugar in baking and has no aftertaste. **Note:** Some people DO have reactions to large amounts of Erythritol.
* **MONKFRUIT EXTRACT:** Monkfruit extract is awesome-sauce. It is a 100% natural sweetener made from an extremely sweet asian melon. Most people who have allergies or sensitivities to artificial sweeteners can have monkfruit extract without any problems. *Monkfruit In The Raw* has a very slight aftertaste. **Note:** Some brands of monkfruit extracts are cut with Erythritol, like the "Lakanto" brand, which has no aftertaste.

For most of you folks that cook a lot and have spent years trying new things in the kitchen, these Gadgets & Gizmos are nothing new to you. But this particular page is directed more towards people who aren't as comfortable in the kitchen yet and are wondering what some of the things are that I mention a lot in my posts. I've often heard people say "what's a food processor,?" or "Immersion Blender?" Well I thought it'd be a good use of a page to point out what some of the primary things are that I use, and what their purpose is, for the newer cooks in the kitchen.

1. Food Processor

Food processors are incredibly versatile I use them for everything from making hummus and creamy mashed cauliflower and tomatillo sauces, to chopping & shredding veggies and quickly "grinding" meats. I've even used it to make pasta and bread dough.

Have a cream sauce with yogurt in it that curdled? Throw it in a processor or blender for a few seconds. Hate lumpy mashed cauliflower? Spoon it in with a little liquid, turn it on and get it as smooth as the creamiest mashed potatoes in a few seconds.

2. Pasta Makers

Seriously folks, I know it sounds intimidating and scary just THINKING about making fresh pasta for the first time, but once you have it, you'll NEVER go back. Fresh pasta is lower in points than store bought dried pasta and is very easy to accurately portion. You can have 1 easily proportioned serving of pasta for 3sp, where you're looking at 5sp for store pasta per serving. It adds up fast.

3. Wire Strainers

These get used a lot when making sauces to strain out the solids and leave the liquids behind. Also great for dusting the top of desserts or dishes. Make sure to have 1 "Fine" wire mesh, even if it's a little one. They don't need to be expensive. Mine are from Target and the 99 cent store.

4. Immersion Blender

Of all of the kitchen gadgets that I have, my immersion blender is used more than any of them. I always need to blend or puree something, but just hate the idea of having to drag out my gigantic food processor or unwieldy blender. An immersion blender is essentially a tiny twirling blade at the end of a wand. Stick the immersion blender into a tall container, a pot, into anything that contains ingredients you need to puree/blend without having to first pour them into another container. It's FANTASTIC for pureeing a batch of creamy mashed cauliflower, smoothies, baby food, anything you could want.

5. Stock Pot with Steamer Inserts

This sounds like something that would be crazy expensive, but I've seen them at Ross and Marshalls for $20-$30. They are so worth it. I use the deep insert to steam cakes inside of a Corningware ceramic round dish, as well as using it to steam my Weight Watchers friendly Tamales and Seafood Boils (shrimp, corn, 0sp sausage). I use the shallower steamer insert to steam 2 ingredient dough for Bahn Mi bread and my Asian Steamed Boas. You can also use them together as a 2 tiered steamer. Steam some veggies on the top and shellfish in the deep insert. These have a ton of uses, and lastly, you get an additional large pot which is always a good thing.

Ground Turkey Seasoning Guide

Transforming Extra Lean Ground Turkey

Breakfast Sausage - 0sp (per serving)

Yields: 4 cups
Serving Size: 1/2 cup
Servings 1-8 = 0sp

- 1 lb extra lean ground turkey
- 1/2 tsp salt
- 1/2 tsp fresh ground pepper
- 1 tsp dried sage
- 1 tsp dried thyme
- 1 tsp ground fennel seed
- 1 tsp onion powder
- 1 tsp dried marjoram
- 2 tsp brown sugar
- 1/2 tsp smoked paprika
- 3 Tbsp plain ff yogurt (or greek)
- 1 Tbsp SF Maple Syrup (OPTIONAL)
- 1/8-1/4 tsp cayenne pepper to taste **(OPTIONAL)**

- Combine all ingredients in a mixing bowl, mix well
- Form into 16 separate 1/4 cup patties
- Use cooking spray to pan fry the patties for 8-10 minutes, turning to brown both sides

NOTE: You can make your own ground fennel seed using a CHEAP coffee/spice grinder from ebay, I got mine for $8.

Italian Sausage - 0sp (per serving)

Yields: 4 cups
Serving Size: 1/2 cup
Servings 1-8 = 0sp

- 1 lb extra lean ground turkey
- 1 tsp ground fennel seed
- 1/2 tsp garlic powder
- 1/2 tsp onion powder
- 3 Tbsp plain ff yogurt (or greek)
- 1 tsp dried italian herbs
- 1/2 tsp dried basil
- 1 Tbsp dried parsley
- 1/4 tsp salt
- 1/4 tsp fresh ground pepper
- 3/4 tsp paprika
- 2 Tbsp red wine vinegar
- 1 Tbsp beef or chicken granules (bouillon)
- red pepper flakes to taste (OPTIONAL)

- Combine all ingredients in a mixing bowl, mix well
- Use cooking spray to pan fry the mixture over medium heat until browned, breaking up meat with spoon.

NOTE: You can make your own ground fennel seed using a CHEAP coffee/spice grinder from ebay, I got mine for $8.

Ground Chorizo Sausage - 0sp (per serving)

Yields: 4 cups
Serving Size: 1/2 cup
Servings   1 = 0sp
*   2-5 = 1sp*
*   6-8 = 2sp*

- 1 lb extra lean ground turkey
- 3 Tbsp plain ff yogurt (or greek)
- 3 tsp minced garlic (3 med. cloves)
- 1 Tbsp chili powder
- 2 tsp paprika
- 1/2 tsp smoked paprika
- 3/4 tsp salt
- 1/2 tsp fresh ground pepper
- 1 tsp dried oregano
- 1/2 tsp cayenne pepper *(OPTIONAL)*
- 1/2 tsp ground cumin
- 1/2 tsp ground coriander
- 1/4 tsp ground cinnamon
- 1 Tbsp beef granules (bouillon)
- 2 Tbsp apple cider vinegar **

- Combine all ingredients in a mixing bowl, mix well
- Use cooking spray to pan fry the mixture over medium heat until browned, breaking up meat with spoon.

NOTE: This is a non spicy MILD chorizo mix if made without the cayenne pepper. You can add more to taste.

Savory Ground Turkey - 0sp (for the entire pound)

Yields: 4 cups
Serving Size: 1/2 cup
Servings 1-8 = 0sp

- 1lb extra lean ground turkey
- 3 Tbsp plain ff yogurt (or greek)
- 3 tsp beef flavored granules
- 1 tsp onion powder
- 1 tsp garlic powder
- 1/2 tsp smoked paprika
- 1/2 tsp ground cumin
- 1 tsp low sodium soy sauce
- 2 tsp worcestershire sauce

- Combine all ingredients in a mixing bowl, mix well
- Use cooking spray to pan fry the mixture over medium heat until browned, breaking up meat with spoon.
- Salt and pepper to taste

NOTE: Savory Ground Turkey is a great stand in for ground beef in meatloaves, casseroles, shepherds pie, burgers...

NOTE: If you are following a Kosher or Dairy Free diet you can substitute unsweetened Almond Milk in place of Yogurt

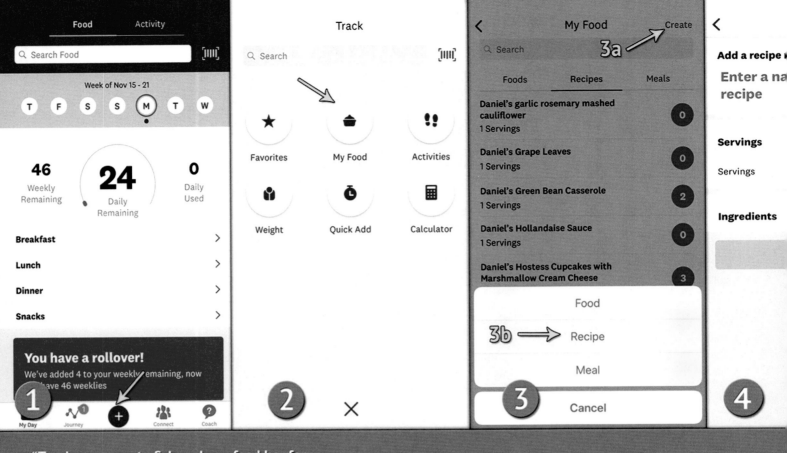

> "Teach a woman to fish and you feed her for a day, teach her to use the recipe builder and you've given her cheesecake."
> — *The Book of Freestyle 8:1*

MASTERING

One of the first rewards that I set for myself, was that if and when I'd lose my first 20lbs, that I could have my mom's old chicken divan casserole. Only one problem, I didn't have the recipe. So I went onto the food network's website and found the recipe from a very famous Southern Chef that loves her some butter. I decided that I would use that for my Chicken Divan.

I opened up the App's Recipe Builder, entered in the recipe exactly as is, and couldn't believe that 1 single serving was 18 points. NO WAY was I going to eat that. I set about trying to make a healthier version and it completely changed everything. I was able to get that casserole down to 2 points per serving from her 18. It was my "Road to Damascus" moment with Weight Watchers.

I am going to do my absolute best in this section to help walk you through a step by step tutorial of how to do what I do with recipes I want to make WW Friendly. I'm going to talk you through how to enter that same chicken divan recipe that I found online, so that we can modify it together.

My HOPE is that it will light the flame in you to start looking at how to manipulate recipes like I do. That way you'll never feel deprived anymore on-program. You'll know how to use the tools that we have been given by WW to make low point, low calorie, low fat, yet delicious, versions of foods that you don't want to give up.

Recipe Builder 101

Alright folks, like I said, I'm going to do my best to help you get the fullest benefit out of the Recipe Builder. So, class is in session. For the benefit of the newer folks to the program, I'm going to type this out as if you have NEVER opened up the Recipe Builder in the app before.

NOTE: The process for adding recipes is very similar from your desktop computer on the WW website. On your computer click the "create" button to the right of the search bar on your desktop.

STEP 1: When you open the app on your mobile device, click the blue circle at the bottom of the screen with the white **+** sign.

STEP 2 & 3: On the next screen click "My Food", followed by (3a) *"Create"* and then (3b) *"Recipe"*, which will take you to the screen that will allow you to begin actually entering in all of the ingredients and serving information.

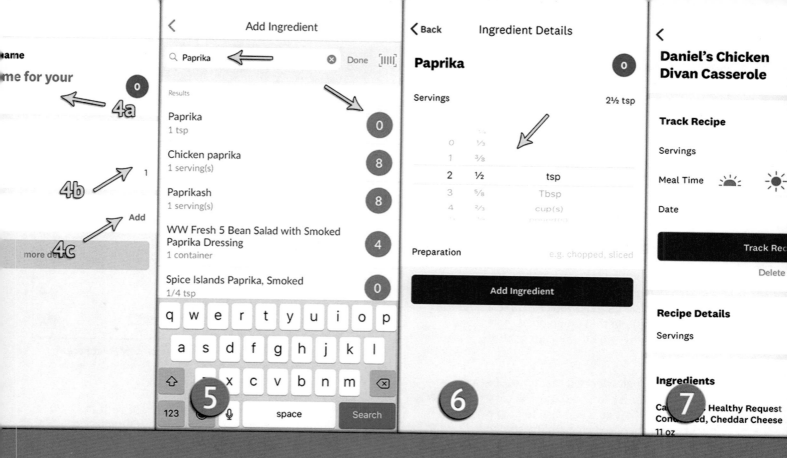

THE RECIPE BUILDER

Practicing the principles of this section will completely change your weight loss journey

STEP 4: Alright, now's where the fun begins. (4a) is where you enter in the name of whatever you'd like your recipe to be called. (4b) is where you input the number of servings. The more servings you can get out of a dish, the further you stretch it's points and the fewer points per serving it becomes in most cases. If a dish has 30 points of ingredients in it and only 1 serving, then it's 30sp per serving. But if that recipe makes 6 servings then it's 5sp per serving. Lastly, (4c) is where the bulk of your time will be spent, adding ingredients. Pressing "add ingredient" takes you to...

STEP 5: Type in the name of an ingredient, in this case we'll search for Paprika. The spice paprika may not be the first thing that pops up and sometimes you need to scroll down to find the item for which you are looking.. A prime example is Pepper, if you search to add Pepper you have to scroll down to find it between items like "black pepper chicken" "pepper jelly" and 30 other things. You'll often need to hunt for the ingredient you really want, but you'll eventually find it or one like it that you can use. Here we'll select Paprika.

STEP 6: Now that you've selected Paprika as your ingredient to add, the program is going to have you enter how much of it you're going to use in the recipe. For a lot of spices it doesn't matter. They stay "0" regardless of whether you use 1tsp or 1/2c of it, there's no change. However, there

are a lot of spices and ingredients that scale up in points, depending on how much you use. This is where you get to really go to town with hacking recipes. But that's later. For now we're just going to add in an entire recipe as is, with all of it's suggested ingredients, measurements and servings.

Recipe Exercise #1

Create a new recipe and name it "AA - TEST RECIPE" so that it's easy to find and delete later. List it as having 8 servings and input the following ingredients and measurements. Do not choose "light sour cream" "reduced fat mayo" etc, use the full fat regular versions of everything. This exercise is to prove a point.

- 20oz Broccoli, cooked
- 6 cups shredded chicken, cooked
- 2 cans of condensed cream of mushroom soup
- 1 cup mayonnaise
- 1 cup sour cream
- 1 cup shredded cheddar cheese
- 1 tablespoon lemon juice
- 1 teaspoon curry powder
- 1/2 cup white wine
- 3/4 cup grated Parmesan
- 1/2 cup plain breadcrumbs
- 3 tablespoons butter

Recipe Builder

Let the Swapping Begin

For purposes of this tutorial, to make it as simple as possible, I am not going to be using things like the fat free cheese hack. We are going to use regular reduced fat cheese and other items that you can easily purchase from the store. So... let's dig in.

Pictured to the right is the in-app point values for most of the ingredients of the original recipe as listed on the previous page. Your mission, should you choose to accept it, is to swap out and substitute these high point ingredients with lower point items that would work just as well.

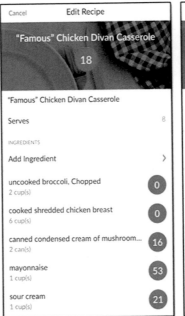

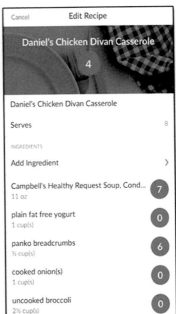

Original Recipe	Revised Low Point Recipe

STEP 1: First thing first. I decided that for me personally that I wanted the chicken, cheese and broccoli casserole to be extra cheesy. To further that goal and also to drop the points I replaced the regular condensed cream of mushroom soup with "heart healthy" Campbell's condensed cream of cheddar cheese soup. This is only 7sp for 2 cans, removing 9 points from the recipe. Next was the ridiculous 74 points from the 1 cup of Mayo and 1 cup of Sour Cream. Those had to go. What do we all use that's white, thick, creamy and goopy? Yup, plain fat free yogurt and plain fat free Greek yogurt. I like to use Greek in place of mayo because it's thicker and plain yogurt in place of sour cream, because it's creamier. 1 cup of each gets rid of 74 more points from the recipe.

STEP 2: Let's get cheesy!!!!

The regular recipe calls for 1 cup of regular shredded cheddar cheese, and 3/4 cups of grated Parmesan cheese. We are going to lower the heck out of that and also up the cheese factor. First, we're going to get rid of those 23 points of cheese and replace them with 1/2 cup of reduced fat shredded cheddar and 1/2 cup of low moisture shredded mozzarella for only 10 points. Using a 1/2-1/2 mix of cheddar and mozzarella will help because we'll still get the cheddar flavor and color, and

STEP 2: *(continued)*
the melted mozzarela will help melt the cheese with the fat free yogurts, helping to prevent curdling. Lastly, we'll replace the 3/4c of grated Parmesan with Grated Reduced Fat Parmesan for 6 points. You can see how all of these subs are quickly making this casserole MUCH healthier, MUCH lower in points and MUCH lower in total fat and calories. But wait, we're not done.

STEP 3: Now we're coming into the home stretch, we're at the liquids. So we'll need water for the condensed soup, that's 2 cups of water. Next is the lemon juice which isn't a problem, then the White Wine. Now, we just want the flavor of white wine in the dish. It can be subtle, it doesn't need to kick us in the face. So do you want a slight flavor?.. Try adding just 1 tablespoon of it in with water. The recipe asks for a 1/2 cup of white wine. Nope... sorry Charlie. We're going to put in 7 tablespoons of additional water, which is 1 tablespoon shy of 1/2 cup... and then we're going to add our 1 tablespoon of wine to it. We end up with 1/2 cup of liquid that has a subtle taste of white wine for 0 points. If you want to bump it up to 2 tablespoons, fine, but for this exercise we're keeping it at 0 points.

Now, because we have all of this liquid, we don't want our sauce to be runny. We'd like it to be thick, creamy and cheesy, so what do we do to thicken it without added heavy cream? Cornstarch. We are going to take 1 and 1/2 tablespoons of cornstarch (1 point), dissolve it in just a tiny bit of water and then stir that in with all of our liquid. We're also going to replace the 15 points of regular butter with 4 points of "I Can't Believe It's Not Butter Light".

The purpose of this exercise is to open your eyes to just how easy it is to make low calorie, low fat, low point versions of regular recipes. Practice doing this a few times with random recipes you find and it will become a game to you. You may need to adjust cooking temps and times occasionally to account for lower fat ingredients, but you'll get the hang of it with a little trial and error.

Recipe Exercise #3

"Healthy" Slow Cooker Meatloaf
Servings: 8
Freestyle/Smart Points: **8**

Ingredients:
Filling: (54 points)
- 1/2 cup   Tomato Sauce - **0sp**
- 2 large   Eggs, beaten - **0sp**
- 1/4 cup   Ketchup - **3sp**
- 1 tsp   Worcestershire Sauce - **0sp**
- 1 small   Onion, chopped - **0sp**
- 1/3 cup   Crushed Saltines (10 crackers) - **4sp**
- 3/4 tsp   Garlic, minced - **0p**
- 1/4 tsp   Seasoning Salt - **0sp**
- 1-1/2 lbs.   90% Lean Ground Beef - **30sp**
- 1/2 lb.   Reduced-Fat Pork Sausage - **17sp**

Sauce: (15 points)
- 1/2 cup   Ketchup - **7sp**
- 3 tbsp   Brown Sugar - **8sp**

WHAT WOULD I DO? *(with basic swaps):*
Modified Points: 0 points per serving !!!!!!
(minus 61 total ingredient points)

Filling: (-49 points)
- Replace ground beef with 1 pound of "Savory Ground Turkey" from page 15. *(-30 points)*
- Replace pork sausage with "Italian Sausage" from page 15. *(-17 point)*
- Reduced sugar ketcup instead of regular *(-2 points)*

Sauce: (-12 points)
- Replace regular Ketchup with Reduced Sugar Ketchup. (-5 points)
- Replace Brown Sugar with 3 Tbsp. Sugar Free Maple Syrup (-7 points)

Recipe Exercise #2

Old Fashioned Chicken Pot Pie
Servings: 6
Points: **20 points per serving!!!!!**

Ingredients: 122 total ingredient points
Filling: (35 points)
- 1/3 cup   Butter - **27sp**
- 1/3 cup   All Purpose Flour - **4sp**
- 1 medium   Garlic Clove, minced - **0sp**
- 1/2 tsp   Salt - **0sp**
- 1/4 tsp   Pepper - **0sp**
- 1-1/2 cups Water - **0sp**
- 2/3 cup   Whole Milk - **4sp**
- 2 tsp   Chicken Bouillon Granules - **0sp**
- 2 cups   Cooked Boneless Chicken Breast, Cubed - **0sp**
- 1 cup   Frozen Mixed Vegetables - **0sp**

Crust: (87 points)
- 1-2/3 cups All Purpose Flour - **21sp**
- 2 tsp   Celery Seed - **0sp**
- 8 oz   Cream Cheese, cubed - **36sp**
- 1/3 cup   Cold Butter - **27sp**

WHAT WOULD I DO? *(with basic swaps):*
Modified Points: 4 points per serving!!!!!
(minus 89 total ingredient points)

Filling: (-25 ingredient points)
- Replace Butter with I Can't Believe It's Not Butter Light" *(-19sp)*
- Use 1 Tbsp Cornstarch instead of the All Purpose Floure *(-3 points)*
- Use Almond Milk instead of whole milk *(-3 points)*

Crust: *(-64 ingredient points)*
- Use 1-1/2 cup portion of Yeast Pizza Dough (pg. 34) as the crust for the pot pie, it's not as traditional, but it's a lot healthier *(-64sp)*

FOUNDATIONS

Recipes for miscellaneous food items used as the building blocks for other meals

Ahh food,.. that great comfort to us all. For some of us there are entire trips or vacations where most of it is a blur when we try to remember it years later, but yet we always seem to remember that one meal that we had at that one place we can't remember the name of. Sure everyone remembers that delicous chicken parmigiana or that heavenly pasta dish you had at the stuffy place with the long name. But how many of us actually walk away from a meal like that saying "That meal was amazing, I wonder how they made the tortillas?" or "that pie was fantastic, I wonder if there's a reduced sugar version?"

This section is dedicated to those unsung heroes of the culinary world that sacrifice themselves for the greater good of a recipe. Those valiant few who encapsulate our chicken breasts without asking for any recognition or fame. These food items don't desire lofty titles, they don't want to be the focus of our admiration, they are content to elevate their fellow ingredients above themselves. They are the mailroom worker of the kitchen, the front desk receptionist of our culinary corporation... without them our meals would crumble. So let us take a moment to give thanks and learn how to carefully craft these waistline wonders so that we can use them in our delectable dishes.

"... blessed be the lowly ingredients that lay the
foundation for great low point meals and treats..."
- The Book of Freestyle 7:30

Foundation Recipes

2 Ingredient Dough

The simple yet versatile dough recipe that keeps us sane

If you've been in-program for any length of time you KNOW how much you missed your bread when you first started. I'm including this in the book because there are a lot of new people who still view 2 ingredient dough as a mystery and ask in Connect "How do you make it? What's in it?" For you new folks, this dough is so incredibly versatile, it truly is the kitchen chameleon. I use this stuff for everything. breakfast pizzas, bagels, steamed for Asian inspired dumplings, thrown it into a hearty low point chicken and dumplings, strombolis, biscuits, impromptu projectiles, the list goes on and on.

Ingredients:

- 1 cup Self Rising flour
- 1 cup Fat Free Plain Greek Yogurt

Directions:

1 Combine the Flour and Yogurt in a mixing bowl until well combined and formed into a ball.
2 Remove from bowl and place on cutting board dusted with flour.
3 Basic cooking method:
   Bake at 400 for 18-25 min.

** Cook temp & time vary depending on application

Various Applications:

- Quarter the dough as pictured below, and use the 4 separate 3sp sections for a variety of uses such as 3sp Bagels, Biscuits, flattened into rounds to make 4 small personal sized pizzas, and much more.
- Cut the dough into 1/8th's instead of 1/4's to make small 2-3sp dough balls for use as bread knots, small dessert bread bites and appetizers.
- Roll the dough out into long ropes and slice it into small dumplings for use in low point chicken and dumplings.
- Steam the dough to make asian buns.

- If you roll out the dough ball into 1 large round pizza dough rather than sectioning it into quarters, you can use it to make a regular sized medium pizza or a large sized thin crust pizza.
- Roll out the dough and use it to make calzones and strombolis.
- Use the sectioned dough to wrap low point hot dogs or use "Lil Smokeys" to make guilt-free "pigs in a blanket".
- Another version is "**3 ingredient dough**". Use 2 cups self rising flour, 1 cup yogurt and 2 eggs. Mix together and portion just like normal. It's more airy and fluffy.

(1) 12 Point Serving

(4) 3 Points per servings

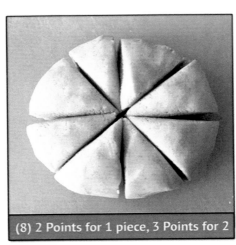

(8) 2 Points for 1 piece, 3 Points for 2

Pizza Dough

If you are looking for a fast, reliable and easy way to make a basic pizza crust that's easy to portion for different amounts of Points, then 2 ingredient dough is a godsend. You can use a 1 cup dough ball to flatten/stretch into a good medium sized thin crust pizza that will only cost 12 points all together in crust. For a comparison, the ready-made pizza dough available at major grocery store chain "*Jrader Toes*" *cough* is over 35 points.

You can also make 4 personal sized pizzas out of the 1 cup dough ball by cutting it into equal 1/4's, each one being 3 Points. When rolled out they are each the size of a personal sized pizza. Or if you want a Small sized pizza, simply cut the dough ball in 1/2 for 2 small pizzas that are 6 points for each crust. Though cook times vary depending on each person's preference, typically everyone bakes their 2 ingredient pizzas at 425 degrees for between 20-25 minutes, depending on how they like their crust.

Bagels, Biscuits, and Preztels

For those of us that aren't nutcase carb-cutters like some of the trend "diets" turn you in to, using 2 ingredient dough to make bagels, biscuits and pretzels is a game changer in our weight loss journey. For regular sized bagels, biscuits, and pretzels you should quarter the 1 cup dough ball, making (4) 3 point sections. For bagels, roll each section into a thick rope and then twist it into a round bagel shape. Pretzels are prepared in the same way except the rope of dough is twisted into a pretzel shape. You can then spray each piece with butter flavored cooking spray, sprinkled it with your desired seasonings and bake. You can also just take the 4 separate quarters, roll them into rounds and then place those into cupcake/muffin baking pans that have been sprayed with cooking spray to make biscuits.
Typical baking & cook time for this application is: 350 degrees for 20 minutes, then turn up the heat to 450 degrees for a final 2-3 minute to brown the top a little more.

Snack Sized Bites

Other than pizzas and big delicious bagel sized fluffy goodness, there are even more ways to utilize this dough. Rather than sectioning it into (4) 3 point sections, you can section the 1 cup dough ball into 8 separate smaller point sections. 1 piece is 2 points, 2 pieces is 3 points and each additional section scales up accordingly (+1 point, +2 points, +1 point).

You can use these smaller sections for a ton of different small bites and appetizer ideas such as bite sized pretzel nuggets, rolling the rounds in your sweetener of choice and cinnamon, form the sections into small flat tortilla-like rounds with a filling in the center and then roll them up into a stuffed bread ball with any number of fillings.. the options are endless. Cooking temperatures and bake times vary depending on what type of snack sized appetizer you are trying to make. A quick search online or in Connect will find tons of recipe ideas.

Empanadas/Stuffed Pockets

2 ingredient dough is also a fantastic vehicle to make savory stuffed breads and pastries. Using the same exact principles as all of the other applications, you can simply fold your preferred filling of choice inside two layers of the dough to make sweet or savory stuffed empanadas, calzones, stromboli, baked panini sandwiches, baked breakfast pockets filled with scrambled eggs, cheese, veggies... you are only bound by the limits of your culinary imagination.

You can find hundreds of delicious recipes and ideas on Connect or any number of websites such as pinterest, emilybites and skinnytaste.

@mappleby777

@mugglemama2017

@julieo145

@mappleby777

Low Point Breading

Sometimes You Have To Get Creative To Game The System

Guilt Free Breading

I'll be the first to admit that I went a little crazy-overboard during my weight loss phase of my journey. I went nearly half a year without eating anything that was breaded because of how point conscious/paranoid I was. Then one day after reaching goal, a thought occured to me. In the recipe builder I noticed that if I added 2tsp of all purpose flour to a recipe it was 1 point, but if I added 2 different types of flour with 1-1/2tsp of EACH, that it was still 0 points even though I now had 3tsp of flour. So that made me go into the builder to see how I could outsmart it with amounts of different crumbs. This is the result.

Ingredients:

- 2 Large Eggs
- 1 Tbsp Water
- 1 Tbsp Fat Free Plain Yogurt (or Greek)
- 1 tsp Dijon Mustard (optional)
- 2/3 cups Instant Mashed Potato Flakes
- 4 tsp Panko Bread Crumbs
- 3 tsp Plain Bread Crumbs
- Additional Herbs & Seasonings to Taste
- Cooking Spray

Serving Size:

Makes enough breading to coat 4 medium sized chicken breasts

Points Value:

1 point per breaded chicken breast

COOKING TIP:

If baking, for best results bake the breaded cutlets on a wire rack on top of your baking pan to allow for heat to circulate around all sides of the chicken. It will keep the bottom of the meat raised off of the surface so that it gets crispy on both sides.

Directions:

1. Whisk together the eggs, water, yogurt, & mustard (if using), in a wide bowl or dish.
2. In a separate container, mix together the flakes, bread crumbs, desired herbs and seasonings.
3. Pat your prepared meat dry with paper towels if necessary to ensure that they are dry.
4. Lightly dredge your meat cutlets, 1 at a time, through the egg-wash, lifting it up and allowing excess eggwash to run back into the bowl.
5. Place the meat into the dish with your breading and lightly coat both sides.
6. Place the breaded meat on a dish and liberally coat with cooking spray on both sides.
7. Cook the breaded meat according to your recipes directions.

How To Make It Melt

There has always been one constant truth in the Universe, that Fat Free Cheese can't melt. Actually it can, it's just always done a really bad job of melting. (It sucks at it, actually.)

One afternoon while cooking I accidentally dropped some fat free cheese on the kitchen counter and it landed up against a little dab of yogurt. I was feeling lazy and decided to clean it up later. However when I came back, the two had kind of melded together, which gave me the idea to try this.

By mixing ANY amount of fat free shredded cheese with roughly 1/2 as much fat free plain or greek yogurt, then using it as a spread, you can "cheese" a pizza, lasagna, casserole, any dish you want, for virtually no points compared to regular cheese. It sounds so wrong... but it's so right. Once exposed to high heat, the yogurt and cheese both melt together..

Fat Free Cheese Hack

How To Make Fat Free Cheeses Melt Like Regular Cheese

Ingredients:

- Any amount of Fat Free Shredded Cheese
- Roughly 1/2 to 3/4 as much Fat Free Plain or Greek Yogurt

Directions:

1 Take any amount of Fat Free Shredded Cheese *(or low fat cheese if you would like to make that more melty as well)* and mix it in a mixing bowl with the yogurt until well combined into a thick ricotta-like sticky mixture.
2 Spread or dollop the cheese onto the surface of the dish you would like it to melt on. Cook in the same manner that you would regular cheese. (IE: Baked into a casserole, on top of Chicken Parmesan, etc)

COOKING TIPS:

- A huge benefit of this versus just rinsing off the cheese to help it melt is that the yogurt adds volume to the cheese, stretching it further in your recipe. Add 1 cup of yogurt to 2 cups of cheese. You now have 3 cups of cheese spread for the points of 2 cups.
- The "Point" value for this technique is based entirely upon how much fat free cheese you decide to use. The Yogurt has 0 points, so all that you are accounting for when building your recipe to determine points-per-serving is the cheese.

Cream Cheese

Turning MILD Greek Yogurt into a 0sp Cream Cheese Sub

DIY Fat Free "Cream Cheese" Substitute

First off I need to give credit where it's due and thank "*@mickeydoyle5*" from Connect for tipping me off to this ingredient hack that I had never heard of before. Once I heard about it I HAD to try it considering how much fat free cream cheese I go through with my cupcakes. THIS STUFF IS AWESOME!!! Make sure that you use a Greek Yogurt with a very mild "tang" to it, as a lot of Greek Yogurts have a very sharp taste that sucks the life & happiness out of desserts normally. I used Chobani Fat Free Greek Yogurt, though my ABSOLUTE FAVORITE is FAGE 0%, Fage is a little pricier but it has the least amount of yogurt tang of all the major brands. It is an almost perfect match to a slightly softened cream cheese with juuuust a tiny bit of bite to it. I personally think that it works as a wonderful sub for cream cheese in dips, spreads and in appetizers. Some folks have been using this in cheesecake recipes with success, which inspired me to start using it in place of cream cheese for my frostings.

Yields: 3.5 cups of Cream Cheese Substitute
Points: 0 Points

What You'll Need:

- 35oz FAGE (or other mild) Fat Free Greek Yogurt
- Cheese Cloth
- Strainer
- Large Bowl
- Plastic Wrap

Directions:

1. Attach or set a plastic or metal strainer onto a large bowl or pot in such a way that the strainer will not come in contact with any liquid that drips to the bottom.
2. Line the bowl of the strainer with 6-8 layers of cheesecloth.
3. Pour all of the Greek Yogurt onto the cheesecloth.
4. Cover it all with plastic wrap and set in the refrigerator for at least 24 hours (mine was fine at 24).
5. Store in an air tight container for up to 1 week and use in place of regular cream cheese.

Note:

- If you are unable to get cheese cloth you can line your strainer with a few layers of paper coffee filters.

0 point creamy awesomeness

Low Point Crust

Replacing Traditional Graham Cracker Crusts for Pies

One of the hardest things to manage while trying to eat healthier is desserts. Let's face it, it's the biggest hurdle for most of us, we love our sweets. Chief among those is pie, traditionally made with a ton of crushed graham crackers, sugar and butter. Regular Graham Cracker pie crust is a freaking Calorie Bomb, and as such is a ton of points. A typical graham cracker pie crust for a 9" pie will add around 55-70 points to your recipe, making it virtually impossible to have pies without blowing through all of your dailies. Well, you can still have pie crust, you just have to get creative and make some compromises.

As with all of this weird stuff I stumble upon, it's all born out of a desire to continue eating the foods I want, period. So, who would know how to knock the points from sugar and butter out of a dessert? Diabetics. I started searching through Diabetic cooking sites and forums and saw that they tended to use low sugar, high fiber cereals for their pie crusts instead of graham crackers. Turns out those are a lot less points than graham crackers too. After a few attempts, this is what I came up with.

Ingredients:

- 1-1/4 cups Kelloggs All Bran Cereal, All Bran Buds, Fiber One, or other low point High Fiber cereal
- 1/2 cup Fat Free Plain Yogurt (or Greek)
- 1/2 tsp ground cinnamon
- 1-1/2 Tbsp Sugar Free Maple Syrup
- 2 tsp Molly Mcbutter Butter Sprinkles (optional)
- 1/4 cup Sweetener of Choice (Monkfruit, Splenda, Stevia, etc)

Servings:

- Makes enough crust for a 9 in. Pie Pan
- 7 Total points for the entire crust

Directions:

1 Put the cereal in a food processor, blend on high until the cereal is processed into a finely ground mixture resembling crushed graham crackers.
2 Add the remaining ingredients and blend on high until well combined.
3 Spray a 9" pie pan or springform pan with cooking spray.
4 Press mixture down into pie pan and compress slightly. with your hands & fingers.
5 Cook the same as you would a regular graham cracker crust.

COOKING TIPS:
- This crust is not nearly as sweet as traditional graham cracker crusts that we are all used to. However if you want it sweeter feel free to add additional sweetener or real sugar. Make sure to adjust your points accordingly.
- After you first process everything together in the food processor, try a tiny taste of it to see if you want to adjust the sweetness or add additional flavorings.

Masa & Tortillas

The Latin American Dough For Tortillas, Tamales, Sopes, & more

Latin American cuisine would be nowhere without Masa, a dough made from very finely ground corn, which is used to make Tortillas, Tamales, Gorditas, Sopes... it is everything in Latin cooking. Think of it like the all purpose flour that you're used to using for the biscuits, rolls, pizza dough, and all other baked goodies that you're used to in western cooking. The flour required to make Masa is in most all grocery stores, typically found in either the Latin/Ethnic section or by where the Cornmeal is sold. Note,.. this is NOT a traditional recipe, this is my version. I like my tortillas a little softer, so I add yogurt in place of lard. Making the masa softer also greatly helps the texture should you choose to make tamales by adding the additional baking powder.

Ingredients:

- 2 cups Masa Harina, Maseca, or other brand Instant Corn Masa (corn flour NOT cornmeal!!)
- 1-1/4 cup Water
- 1/2 cup Fat Free Plain or Greek Yogurt
- 1/2 tsp salt
- Additional water if needed for mixing
  *** (add 2tsp baking powder if being used to make Tamales)

Directions:

1. In a large mixing bowl, combine the corn flour, 1-1/4 cups water, yogurt, and salt. Mix thoroughly until you form a semi-firm dough ball. If dough appears dry while mixing, add additional water as needed.

SERVING SIZE & POINTS:

- Varies. The servings and points for tortillas made in this manner are completely dependant upon how many you make from your dough. It is portioned exactly the same as you would 2 ingredient dough.

2. Remove dough to a cutting board, and cut into 2 equal sized 1 cup dough balls. Then portion each 1 cup dough ball in to 1/4's and then into 1/8's sized portions.

3. Roll each one of the 16 small dough sections into a circular ball. Then, use your palm to press the dough balls into tortilla sized rounds on a cutting board using your fingers and palms to make them into fairly circular shapes.

4. For perfectly uniform and quick tortillas, you can use a traditional tortilla press to form them. They are fairly inexpensive and can be purchased at most swap meets, ethnic grocery stores, or online for around $10.-15. Metal ones are best.

5. To cook, heat a skillet, griddle, or large pan on medium-high heat. Cook each tortilla for around 45 seconds on each side.

6. Keep tortillas warm by placing them in a covered container, or place them on a plate covered with a dish cloth. Tortillas are best served warm.

A FEW DIFFERENT USES:

A) Sopes - Traditionally, the base is made from a circle of fried masa with sides pinched up to resemble a shallow cup. However for WW purposes you should spray it with cooking spray and then bake it. This can then be topped with any number of toppings. Bake the shells at 350 degrees for 10-15 minutes.

B) Tamales - If you are a WW member, you can view a video in Connect where I show how to make 3 point Tamales by searching for #dhallakvids and scrolling down to my DIY Tamale video.

C) Arepas - Arepas are awesome. For best results use a 3 point 1/4 cup section of the Masa dough, form it into a 1/2" thick tortilla round. For the non-fried WW version, cook it on a hot griddle or pan for 45 seconds on each side, and then remove it from the heat and slice it ALMOST completely in half down its length like a big pocket. Stuff it with fillings of your choice, then return it to heat.

D) If you need me to explain what a Taco is... put down this book. Put it down. No really, put it down. No food for you.

COOKING TIP:

- You can easily HALF this recipe if you don't want to make a big batch.
- If you plan to make Tamales OR Arepas, make sure to add 1 tsp of baking powder to each cup of flour that you use to help them fluff up a little bit.
- If you would like to NOT use the yogurt in this recipe due to dairy allergies, you can replace it with an equal amount of silken tofu.
- If you would like an even MORE chewie tortilla, you can substitute 1/4 cup of the corn flour with 1/4 cup of all purpose flour. I personally love the texture that way... but I'm a full-on Gringo.
- If you buy a tortilla press, I would recommend a metal one. They are a few dollars more, but they are more durable. I've broken 2 plastic ones from the hinges breaking with too much pressure.
- Instead of a tortilla press you can put one of the balls of masa between 2 layers of plastic wrap and press down with a pot.
- For more savory tortillas add 1/2 tsp garlic and onion powder to the flour.

Pasta Basics

Making Your Own Low Point Pasta Dough & Noodles

Two of the biggest heartaches you hear in Connect are how much people miss their pastas and how many points they blow on pasta dishes. I used to think the same way. I went MONTHS without having pasta because I didn't want to spend the points. Then I started looking into it and realized that making your own pasta is lower in points, calories and carbs, is tastier than store bought dried pasta and you get A LOT more pasta for the points.

Ingredients:

- 2 cups of all purpose flour (or your flour of choice)
- 3 large eggs
- 1/2 tsp salt (optional)
- 2 Tbsp water
- 5 sprays, olive oil cooking spray
  additional water for mixing if required

Directions:

1. In a large mixing bowl or stand mixer, combine the flour, eggs, salt, olive oil cooking spray and 2 Tbsp of water to form a dough ball. The mixture will be dry, so add water as needed to help the dough come together. We aren't adding all of the water all at once because we want to cut down on how much flour we have to use for dusting later on. Wet dough = bad.

2. Remove dough to a cutting board, and cut into 2 equal sized 1 cup dough balls. I typically wrap and keep 1 of them in the freezer so that I can thaw it out and have ready-made pasta dough at a later time. For this recipe, we will assume that you are doing the same.

3. Take 1 of your 1 cup pasta dough balls, and cut it into (4) 1/4 cup portions, just like when you section 2 ingredient dough. Next, roll each one of the 1/4 cup sections into 4 small dough balls.

4. Each one of these 1/4 cup Pasta Dough balls is a perfectly portioned 3sp bundle of pasta bliss. If you want slightly more pasta, roll the 1 cup dough ball into a log, and cut it into 3 equal portions for 4 point 1/3 cup servings rather than the 3 point 1/4 cup servings.

5. Use your hand and a rolling pin to flatten one of the 1/4 cup pasta balls into a roughly rectangular flat shape.

6. You are trying to shape your flattened dough balls to fit length-wise across most of the pasta makers guide-track.

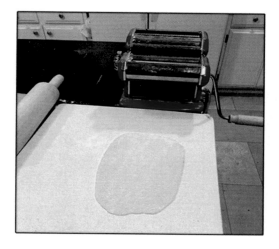

7. With the pasta-width adjustment at its widest setting, run the pasta through the rollers 2 or 3 times, and then adjust the knob on the machine to make the rollers 1 step closer together.

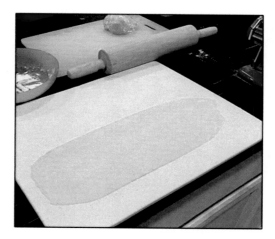

8. After every 2-3 passes through the rollers continue to make the pasta sheet thinner until you stop at the 2nd from the thinnest setting, which is my personal preference.

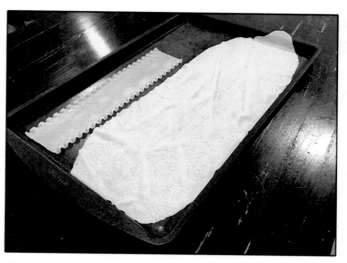

9. Pictured is 3 points of cooked store bought dried lasagna noodles (left) next to the cooked 3 point pasta sheet that we just made

10. This image shows the difference between 12 points of cooked store bought dried spaghetti noodles (right) next to 12 points of cooked fresh Linguini.

COOKING TIP:

- There is no need to dry out the pasta. As soon as you have your noodles just drop them into boiling water for 2-3 minutes. Yep, it cooks that fast.
- If you are making lasagna I would highly recommend boiling the pasta sheets first then rinsing them off. Boiling them will make them expand to be as big as what is pictured in the image above #9 and will give them a slightly firmer texture.
- Aside from tasting better, fresh pasta is lower in calories, carbs and total points than dried store bought pasta per serving.
- If you do not have a stand mixer to mix your dough you can either mix it by hand in a mixing bowl, or you can actually mix the dough VERY quickly in a food processor. Go online and search for "Martha Stewart Food Processor Pasta Dough" to see a video of how to do it. That's how I made my dough prior to getting this stand mixer. It's faster too.
- Though more time consuming, the benefit of a hand crank style pasta maker is that you can adjust the thickness of the pasta. Stand mixer pasta roller attachments also allow you to adjust the thickness of the finished pasta sheets, however stand mixers are expensive. Manual hand crank pasta makers can be found on ebay and amazon for $50.
- Once you taste the difference you will never go back. Especially with the frozen 1c dough balls ready to go in the freezer after they thaw out.

Ricotta Pasta Dumplings

Making fresh Ricotta Gnocchi without special equipment

As much as I enjoy making pasta from scratch, most folks in WW don't make their own pasta. I needed to figure out a way to show people how easy it could be to make their own delicious pasta at home without needing any special equipment. I realized the tough part is that people could make the dough, but they wouldn't be able to actually cut linguini, spaghetti, or other noodle shapes. I needed to think of a work around that wouldn't be intimidating. Now all people have to do is make dough, roll it into ropes, cut it into nuggets and boil. Done.

The KEY to these dumplings is that you want to cut them small. They are not meant to be the bulk of a dish. Fortify them in with a pan with lots of veggies, meats, and sauce so that it stretches the 1/4 cup servings as far as you can. They are the star of a dish, not the bulk of it.

Yields: (2) 1 cup Dough Balls, (8) 1/4 cup servings, around 70 small dumplings per 1/4 cup

Ingredients:

- 2 cups All Purpose Flour *(or your preferred flour)*
- 1 tsp baking powder
- 2 large eggs
- 1/2 cup Fat Free Ricotta Cheese
- 1/2 tsp salt
- olive oil cooking spray
- additional water to mix (around 1/4 cup)

Directions:

3. Cut the 1 cup dough ball section into (4) 1/4 cup, then cut those in half into small 1/8 cup sections.

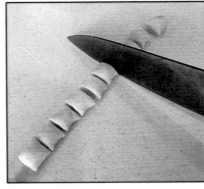

5. Cut each strand into small dumplings. You should be able to get around 25 to 30 per "rope."

1. In a large mixing bowl, combine the flour, baking powder, eggs, ricotta and salt to form a dough ball. Add extra water as necessary to just help the ball come together. The dough should be the texture of semi firm playdough. Not too firm, but still soft.

2. Cut the 2 cup dough ball into 2 equal sized 1 cup dough balls. Wrap one in plastic wrap and store in the freezer for later use if you only want to make a 1 cup batch, otherwise prepare both sections.

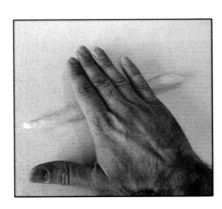

4. Roll out each small dough ball into long "rope" strands about as thick as your pinky finger. Lightly spray with the cooking spray to prevent sticking and avoid adding extra flour.

6. Drop dumplings in to boiling water and cook for 2-3 minutes. Toss with your sauce immediately, or rinse with cold water and store in a ziplock bag in the fridge for later.

Slow Cooker Roasted Garlic

For those of you who are just starting out in the kitchen, or if you just simply haven't tried it before, I hope that I can convert you to the glories of Roasted Garlic. Where regular raw garlic has a sharp bite to it, Roasted Garlic is Raw Garlic's cool cousin that pulls up riding a Harley and blasting "Born In The USA". It has a deep flavor that is much smoother than regular garlic. It's "bite" is so mild that you can even eat it on its own like macho candy without flinching.

As a busy dad who has errands to run, roasting garlic in the oven isn't always practical, so doing it in the slow cooker is perfect. Throw a bunch of garlic in, come back 6 hours later, done.

What You'll Need:

- Slow Cooker
- Whole Heads of Raw Garlic, as many as you want
- Aluminum Foil Wrap
- Olive Oil Cooking Spray
- Pinch of Salt
- Commercial-grade gas mask (optional)

Directions:

1. On a cutting board, use a knife to cut off the top 1/4 to 1/2 inch (depending on size of the garlic) from the top of each head. Remove some of the flaky papery skin from around the garlic.

2. Make an aluminum foil pouch that's at least 2 layers thick (a large piece of foil folded in half, to help avoid burning) and large enough to contain all of the cut heads of garlic.

3. Spray 5 times into the pouch with the olive oil cooking spray, coating all of the heads in a thick layer, then close the foil pouch. Leave a small slit or two.

4. Place a small cup or dish on the bottom of your slow cooker, and then place your foil pouch on top of it to help reduce the chance of burning. Cover and cook on the LOW setting for 5 hours.

5. Remove Garlic from the slow cooker and allow it to cool on a cutting board until you can handle it with your bare fingers without screaming like a little girl watching a Boy Band. Squeeze the soft garlic out of the skins, and store in a plastic ziplock bag in the freezer. Break off a few cloves whenever you need some. They thaw very quickly once removed from the freezer.

Notes:

- Regular Roasted Garlic recipes call for a good amount of olive oil to be poured over the top of all of the heads of garlic. This way gives you 0sp deliciously mellow, nutty, garlic without guilt.

- I prefer to have my slow cooker make this in my back yard. If you cook this inside your house for 5 hours your house will smell like a pizza parlor for days.

- Studies have shown that roasting garlic in this manner helps to prevent Vampire nests from forming on/near your property.

- Eating lots of garlic has been shown to work as a repellent for unwanted harassment and physical advances.

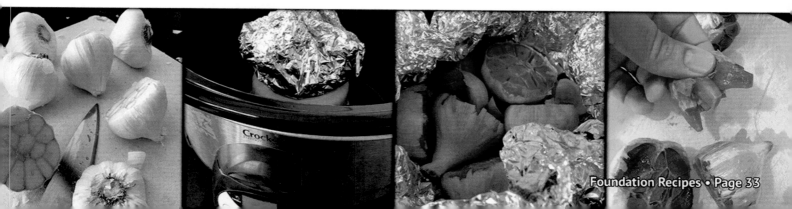

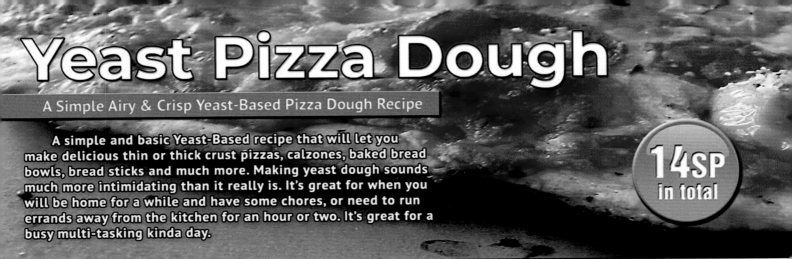

Yeast Pizza Dough

A Simple Airy & Crisp Yeast-Based Pizza Dough Recipe

A simple and basic Yeast-Based recipe that will let you make delicious thin or thick crust pizzas, calzones, baked bread bowls, bread sticks and much more. Making yeast dough sounds much more intimidating than it really is. It's great for when you will be home for a while and have some chores, or need to run errands away from the kitchen for an hour or two. It's great for a busy multi-tasking kinda day.

14SP in total

Ingredients:

- 1 cup All Purpose Flour (or your flour of choice)
- 1/4 tsp Salt (optional if on low sodium diet)
- 1/4 tsp Baking Powder
- 1-1/8 tsp Active Dry Yeast
- 1 tsp Sugar
- 1/2 cup Water, lukewarm

Directions:

1. Combine the flour, salt and baking powder in a large mixing bowl. Set aside

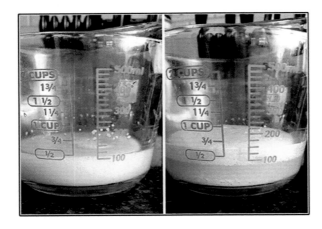

2. In another dish or cup, pour in the active dry yeast and sugar. Pour in the 1/2 cup of lukewarm water then stir for a few seconds to mix. Allow the yeast water to sit untouched for 15 minutes. In that time the yeast water will develop a frothy "head" to it.

3. After 15 minutes, pour the yeast mixture into the mixing bowl with the dry ingredients. Mix to combine until a dough ball is formed, adding a bit more water if the mix is still too dry. It's ok if it's a little sticky.

4. Lightly spray a bowl with cooking spray and put the dough ball in, then cover the bowl with plastic wrap. Walk away and allow the dough to rise for 30 minutes. By that time, it will have expanded and fluffed up a bit.

5. Remove the dough and place it onto the center of a pizza pan that has been lightly sprayed with cooking spray. Stretch out the dough to a large round shape, spray the top with cooking spray and allow it to rest for 1 hour uncovered.

6. After 1 hour the dough has risen a good deal, lightly spray the dough with olive oil cooking spray and gently stretch it more.

7. Put your sauce, cheese and toppings onto the pizza and allow it one final rest for 30 minutes. Turn on your oven to 400.

8. After your pizza has had the additional 30 minutes to rise and has been topped, get ready to put it into your preheated oven.

9. Lightly spray the visible crust with cooking spray, then put your pizza in the oven and bake at 400 degrees for 20-25 minutes.

10. Bask in the glory of real pizza dough.

COOKING IDEAS:

- If you make a double batch of this dough you can make an AWESOME deep dish pizza in a 13"x9" casserole pan, using the exact same method listed to make this dough, just with the doubled ingredients.

- If you make a double batch you can also put your dough onto a large baking sheet pan rather than a round pizza pan, roll the dough into a long rectangular shape, then allow it to rise, stretch it more, rise, top it, bake it and you can get up to 18 good sized square slices out of it.

- You can use instant yeast instead of dry active yeast. Rather than adding the active dry yeast to water and waiting 10 minutes as stated in these directions, you can simply add 2-1/2 tsp of instant yeast directly into the flour with the warm water and mix the dough. It will rise when you let the dough ball rest. It saves a little time.

- You can use this to make Calzones, Strombolis, life sized edible statues of your pets... get creative.

- I personally like to add 1/2 tsp of garlic powder, 1/2 tsp of onion powder, 1 tsp of dried thyme and some cracked black pepper into the flour. The finished bread can be used as breadsticks or for paninis.

SAUCES

Never get bored with your meals again thanks to these 30 ultra low point sauces

One of the hardest things to deal with in any healthy eating lifestyle change is simply how much you begin to feel like there is so little that you can eat. You can easily fall into a pattern with your meals of only making the same few dishes over and over, which can eventually be the hardest thing to overcome. Ever heard the old broken record of "I can't take 1 more night of chicken!"? Well, there's hope in the form of a ton of sauces that I'm about to throw at you.

None of the sauces in this section are over 1 point per serving. Unlike most all other "healthy" recipe books or healthy foodie blogger chefs, my serving sizes ARE REALISTIC. There's no place here for a serving size of hummus being 2 tablespoons, or a serving of pesto being a few teaspoons to fudge the point values. We're talking 1/4 cup all the way up to 1 cup servings of sauces for only 0-1 points per serving. THAT's realistic and that's how you make this journey sustainable.

Show people that they don't have to cut their portions in half to enjoy their food. Show them how, with SMART ingredient substitutions, they can cut points and calories in half while keeping portion sizes the same or even increasing them!

I have spent 3 months working on the recipes for these sauces hoping to provide as many as I possibly can so that you can use them as a base to make or modify your own recipes. Between everything earlier in this book and these sauces, you have all you possibly need to completely and utterly dominate your journey and own Freestyle.

"Rejoice!" shouted dhallakx7 "for I come bearing the gift of 0 point Buffalo Sauce for thy chicken wings!"
- The Book of Freestyle 10:8

Section Recipes

SAUCES

Asian Glaze & Dipping Sauce

A thick and sticky dipping sauce that's easily customizable

This is a very simple Asian inspired sauce that can easily be docked up with additional spices and flavorings for your own preferences. This sauce is yummie as listed, but can be kicked up a few notches by adding lemongrass, some lime juice, asian chili sauce, or any number of additional flavors.

Ingredients:

- 5 Tbsp less sodium soy sauce
- 1/4 tsp sugar
- 3 tsp brown sugar
- 1 medium garlic clove, minced (1tsp)
- 1/4 tsp ground ginger
- 1 Tbsp reduced sugar or sugar free BBQ sauce or ketsup
- 1 Tbsp sugar free maple syrup
- 3 tsp apple cider vinegar
- 1-1/4 cups Water
- 1 Tbsp + 1tsp cornstarch
- red pepper flakes or asian chili sauce to taste *(OPTIONAL)*

Serving Info.:

Yields: 2 cups
Servings: 8
Serving Size: 1/4 cup

Points Value:

1-2 servings = 0 point
3-5 servings = 1 point
6-7 servings = 2 point
8 servings = 3 points

Directions:

1. Combine soy sauce, sugar, brown sugar, garlic, ginger, bbq sauce or ketsup, maple syrup, vinegar, water and red chili flakes (if using), in a small pot or saucepan and heat till boiling.
2. Reduce heat to low and allow the sauce to simmer at a low boil for 2 minutes.
3. In a small dish, mix the cornstarch with just enough water to let it dissolve.
4. Stir the cornstarch mixture into the sauce over medium heat, it will begin to thicken immediately. Continue to stir the sauce until it gets nice and thick, around 2 minutes.
5. Turn off heat. Sauce will continue to thicken over time as it cools.
6. Stir sauce again after 5 minutes off of heat, serve warm or cold.

Avocado Cilantro Sauce

A deliciously creamy sauce perfect for meats, veggies and even salads

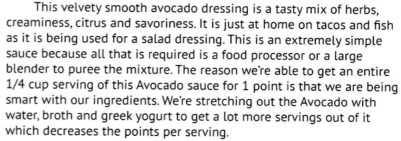

This velvety smooth avocado dressing is a tasty mix of herbs, creaminess, citrus and savoriness. It is just at home on tacos and fish as it is being used for a salad dressing. This is an extremely simple sauce because all that is required is a food processor or a large blender to puree the mixture. The reason we're able to get an entire 1/4 cup serving of this Avocado sauce for 1 point is that we are being smart with our ingredients. We're stretching out the Avocado with water, broth and greek yogurt to get a lot more servings out of it which decreases the points per serving.

The end result is a sauce that is creamy and smooth with a subtle lime flavor, a healthy dose of cilantro and a delicious richness from the Avocado.

Serving Info.:
YIELDS: 2-1/4 cups
Servings: 9
Serving Size: 1/4 cup

Point Values:
1 serving = 1 point
2 servings = 2 points
3 servings = 4 points

Ingredients:
- 1 medium Avocado
- 2 medium garlic cloves
- 1 cup fresh cilantro
- 3 Tbsp lime juice
- 7 Tbsp water
- 1/3 cup chicken broth
- 1 cup plain fat free greek yogurt
- 1/2 tsp salt
- 1/4 tsp pepper
- Olive oil spray, 5 second spray

Directions:
1. Carefully slice the avocado in half, remove the pit and skin, then place the avocado into the food processor.
2. Add all of the remaining ingredients to the food processor and then puree on high speed for around 1 minute, or until all of the ingredients are broken down and smooth.
3. Season with additional salt and pepper, if necessary.
4. Serve immediately or chill in the refrigerator.

Notes:
- This is more of a savory sauce than a bright citrus one. If you would prefer it to have a less savory taste, then replace the chicken broth with additional water. Do not add any pepper, and only season with a minimal amount of salt, to taste, after the rest of the ingredients are finished being pureed.
- Add more water to thin the mixture, if you want a thinner sauce/dressing

Barbecue Sauce

A simple sauce that you can easily modify and build off of

Brush this simple sugar free barbecue sauce on chops, kebabs or chicken drumsticks before cooking, or use as a glaze during grilling. Serve it as either a hot or cold sauce to go with any of your favorite dishes. It's a perfect base to dock up yourself for a low point bbq style sauce. It's so low in points that you have a lot of room to play around with adding ingredients to make it your own.

Ingredients:

- 1/4 cup water
- 2 large onions, chopped
- 4 garlic cloves, medium, chopped
- 1 (29oz) can of tomato sauce (the 0 point kind)
- 1/4 cup worcestershire sauce
- 2 Tbsp apple cider vinegar
- 1/2 cup sugar free maple syrup
- 2 tsp ground mustard
- 1/2 tsp onion powder
- 1 tsp chili powder
- 1 tsp smoked paprika
- 1 tsp paprika
- 1/2 tsp liquid smoke, hickory or mesquite (OPTIONAL)
- salt and pepper to taste

Serving Info.:

Yields: 5 cups
Servings: 20
Serving Size: 1/4 cup

Points Value:

1-2 servings = 0 points
3-7 servings = 1 point
8- 12 servings = 2 points

Directions:

1 In a medium saucepan, saute the onions and garlic with cooking spray, until softened.
2 Stir in all of the remaining ingredients and heat to a low simmer.
3 Cover and simmer for 15 minutes.
4 Pour the mixture into a blender or food processor and process on high until smooth.
5 Return the sauce to the pan and season with additional salt and pepper, if desired.

Variations:
- *This recipe is so low in points that it leaves you a lot of room to customize it to taste exactly how you want. Add some molasses, maybe some brown sugar, soy sauce, honey, the options are endless with this many points to play with.*
- *This sauce is also so low in points that you can easily substitute the sugar free maple syrup for real syrup, though you will have to adjust the points accordingly.*

Bearnaise Sauce

A Classic French Herbed Wine Sauce For Meat Eaters

A classic French sauce gets a low point makeover in this lightened version of one of the most classic French "mother" sauces. Typically, it is made with an emulsion of egg yolk, white wine, vinegar, herbs and loooots of butter. This sauce is Hollandaise's sophisticated wine drinking older brother.

Ingredients:

- 5 Tbsp white wine vinegar
- 1 Tbsp white wine, chardonnay
- 1 cup water
- 1 small onion, chopped
- 1 bay leaf
- a few sprigs each of fresh parsley and tarragon
- 1/4 tsp cracked black pepper
- 1-1/2 Tbsp I Can't Believe It's Not Butter Light
- 1 tsp cornstarch, dissolved in a little bit of water, set aside
- 3 large egg yolks
- 1 Tbsp finely chopped fresh parsley
- 1 Tbsp finely chopped fresh tarragon

Serving Info.:

Yields: 2 cups
Servings: 8
Serving Size: 1/4 cups

Points Value:

1 serving = 0 points
2-5 servings = 1 point
6-8 servings = 2 points

Directions:

1. Combine the white wine, vinegar, water, chopped onion, bay leaf, pepper, butter spread and the sprigs of fresh herbs in a small stock pot and heat until boiling. Lower the heat to medium/low and keep at a low simmer for 5 minutes.

2. Pour the mixture through a wire strainer so that you are left with only the liquid. Set the bowl aside and allow to cool for 30 minutes on the counter.

3. After cooling for 30 minutes, return the mixture to your sauce pot and whisk in the egg yolks and dissolved cornstarch. Turn on the stove to medium and heat until the sauce begins to warm and thicken, about 5 minutes, stirring with a rubber spatula.

4. Once the sauce comes to a low simmer, reduce the heat to barely simmering and allow to continue simmering for 3 minutes, continue stirring.

5. Pour the thickened sauce into a bowl and stir in the chopped fresh parsley and tarragon. Can be served as a hot or cold sauce.

** *You can substitute 4 teaspoons of Molly Mcbutter butter sprinkles for the "I Can't Believe It's Not Butter Light" to turn this into an ultra low point sauce, 1-3 servings for 0 points.*

Bechamel Sauce

A delicously light and versatile take on a classic French sauce

Bechamel is a creamy base sauce, typically loaded with heavy cream and butter. We are using unsweetened almond milk and molly mcbutter that are infused with vegetables, and herbs to create a simple sauce with a subtle depth of flavor. It has an excellent mellow base, which makes it ideal for lasagnas, as well as an accompaniment for many fish, egg, and vegetable dishes. It can also be used as a base in a wide range of sauces and dishes. Add some garlic and you have a creamy garlic sauce, add lemon and herbs and you have a creamy lemon and herb sauce, the possibilities are endless. I personally like to use it for the white sauce in my low point chicken and vegetable lasagna pictured to the left. It is a much healthier WW-ified take on a major brand's frozen vegetable lasagna that we all know and love.

Ingredients:

- 1/2 cup unsweetened plain almond or soy milk
- 3 cups water
- 3 tsp molly mcbutter fat free butter sprinkles
- 1-1/2 tsp chicken flavored bouillon (granules)
- 1 pinch of nutmeg
- a few sprigs of parsley
- a few sprigs of rosemary or thyme
- 1 small onion, diced
- 1 medium carrot, chopped
- 1 celery stalk, chopped
- 1 bay leaf
- 1/4 cup plain fat free yogurt (or greek)
- 4 Tbsp cornstarch (1/4 cup)
- salt and pepper

Servings:

Makes: 3 cups
Servings: 6
Serving Size: 1/2 cup

Points Value:

1 serving = 1 point
2 servings = 2 points

Notes:

- You can replace the Molly Mcbutter with 2 Tbsp I Can't Believe It's Not Butter Light but you will need to adjust the points per serving in the recipe builder.
- You can also replace the chicken bouillon and 1/2 cup of the water in the recipe for 1/2 cup of chicken broth

Directions:

1. Dice the onion, carrot and celery. Spray a medium stock pot with butter flavored cooking spray and cook the veggies on medium heat for 2-3 minutes, until they begin to sweat.
2. Pour in the water, milk, butter sprinkles, bouillon, nutmeg, along with the fresh herbs and bay leaf. Heat on medium heat until boiling, then remove the pot from heat and allow the mixture to steep for 30 minutes.
3. Pour the cooled mixture through a strainer to reserve the liquid.
4. In a separate bowl, combine the cornstarch and yogurt until smooth, adding a little bit of the sauce to warm up the yogurt.
5. Pour the strained liquid back into the pot and stir in the yogurt/cornstarch mixture, until well combined.
6. Heat the mixture over medium heat, stirring frequently, until it reaches a low boil. Reduce the heat and allow to barely simmer for 3-4 minutes for the sauce to thicken up a bit.
7. Remove the pan from the heat and season to taste.
8. The sauce can be served immediately, or it can be allowed to cool for a few minutes. It thickens more as it cools.

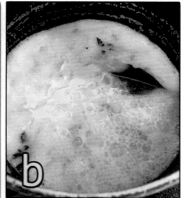

NOTE: All Bechamel variation recipes have the same 1/2 cup serving size as the base sauce.

Bechamel Variations

Bechamel is a perfect base for a number of creamy savory sauces. You can make 1 batch of Bechamel and easily modify it for your own tastes with just a few minor tweaks. For all of these sauces, make a regular batch of Bechamel sauce with the listed changes and additions. This'll show you how easy it is to make your own creations.

Alfredo Sauce:

Prepared by: @ leesha_jay

Points Value: 1 serving = 1 point
2 servings = 3 points

Altered Ingredients/Prep:

- Add 3 chopped cloves of garlic to the vegetables in the first step of the Bechamel sauce.
- Stir in 1/4 cup of reduced fat Parmesan grated topping. (such as Kraft reduced fat Parmesan)

Creamy Herb Sauce:

Prepared by: @ mugglemama2017

Tarragon Sage Chicken with Butternut Squash Soup and Tarragon Sage Cream

Points Value: 1 serving = 1 point
2 servings = 2 points

Altered Ingredients/Prep:

- Replace the Rosemary in the original Bechamel sauce with sprigs of any other herb, such as dill, tarragon, sage, basil, cilantro, etc. and remove during straining.
- Add fresh finely chopped herbs to the finished sauce when it has been strained and thickened. You don't want to cook the chopped herbs or they will discolor.

Lemon & Chive Cream Sauce:

Points Value: 1 serving = 1 point
2 servings = 2 points

Altered Ingredients/Prep:

- Use a small bunch of fresh chives and 1 tsp of lemon peel in place of the rosemary during the first steps of making your Bechamel sauce. Strain as normal.
- Add 2 Tbsp of lemon juice and 3 Tbsp of fresh chopped chives to the finished sauce

Roasted Garlic Cream Sauce:

Prepared by: @ leesha_jay

Points Value: 1 serving = 1 point
2 servings = 2 points

Altered Ingredients/Prep:

- Add 5-6 medium sized cloves of roasted garlic (pg 33) to all of the vegetables when making the Bechamel, along with 1/2 tsp of garlic powder and 1-1/2 Tbsp of reduced fat grated Parmesan topping. Strain out the garlic cloves with the other vegetables.

Black Peppercorn Sauce

A smoky black pepper cream sauce with delicious depth

This sauce tastes so good! It has a savory herbed butter flavor with a smoky pepperiness that sneaks up and karate chops the back of your tongue like an angry creamy ninja. This would be absolutely awesome on beef and pork. Heck, it'd be good as lip balm for goodness sake.

Ingredients:

- 1 small onion, finely diced
- 2 medium cloves garlic, diced
- 5 sprays, butter flavored cooking spray
- 1 Tbsp I Can't Believe It's Not Butter Light
- 1 bay leaf
- 3-4 sprigs fresh thyme
- 1 Tbsp fresh cracked black pepper (coarse if able)
- 1 Tbsp whole black peppercorns
- 1/2 cup chicken broth
- 3/4 cup water
- 1/4 cup plain fat free yogurt, room temperature
- 2 Tbsp unsweetened almond, soy, or fat free/skim milk
- 2 tsp lemon juice
- 3 tsp cornstarch

Serving Info.:

Yields: 2 cups
Servings: 8
Serving Size: 1/4 cups

Points Value:

1 serving = 0 point
2 servings = 1 points
3 servings = 1 points
4 servings = 2 points

Directions:

1. Melt the butter in a pan and cook the onions for 3-4 minutes, until sweating. Add the garlic and cook for 1-2 minutes, until the garlic becomes fragrant.
2. Spray the onions and garlic for 5 seconds with butter flavored cooking spray, add the black pepper, herbs and black peppercorns to the pan and cook on medium-low heat for 3-4 minutes.
3. In a separate bowl, combine the water, chicken broth, yogurt, lemon juice, milk and cornstarch. Whisk together for 1 minute, or until all of the yogurt is dissolved into the liquids and smooth.
4. Pour the liquid mixture into the pan with the onions and pepper, stir constantly with a whisk. Bring the sauce up to a low simmer and continue whisking for 2-3 minutes, until it thickens to your desired consistency. Use a fork to remove the bay leaf and thyme sprigs.
5. Turn off the heat and serve immediately, or allow to cool for a few minutes. The sauce thickens more as it cools.

Notes:

- You can replace the "butter" with 3 tsp of molly mcbutter for a lower point sauce.
- This would be great with sauteed mushrooms added into it which would increase the servings and lower the points accordingly.

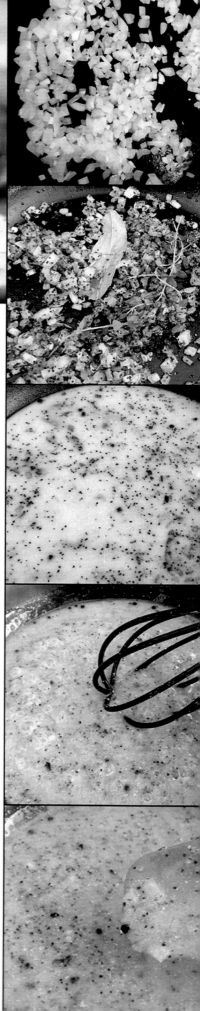

Bolognese & Ragu Sauce

An extremely hearty meat sauce originating from Bologna Italy

A traditional Bolognese sauce is a thing of beauty. Where a Marinara sauce is what you would typically think of when you picture a plate of spaghetti or on a pizza, a Bolognese sauce is much more hearty. The sauce is usually packed with ground beef or pork sausage, but we are going for a low fat, low calorie, low point sauce, so we are using extra lean ground turkey seasoned like Italian Sausage (pg 15). You can easily transform this into a very hearty Ragu sauce by adding some finely chopped carrots, celery, onions and even mushrooms. In this recipe I'm giving instructions for cooking the sauce as a Ragu. If you wish to have a regular Bolognese style sauce you can prepare it the same way, but without the carrots and celery. If you'd like to make your Ragu even heartier, consider adding Mushrooms.

Ingredients:

- 1 pound uncooked "0 point" Italian Sausage (page 15)
- 1 medium onion, diced (around 1-1/2 cups)
- 1/2 cup carrot, finely chopped***
- 1/2 cup celery, finely chopped***
- 4-5 medium garlic cloves, minced
- 2/3 cup low fat beef or chicken broth
- 1 Tbsp red wine vinegar
- 1/4 cup red wine
- 2 Tbsp tomato paste, no salt added
- 29 oz. canned tomatoes, chopped or diced, with liquid
- 1 tsp italian seasoning
- 1/2 tsp rosemary, minced
- 1/4 tsp ground allspice
- salt and pepper to taste

Serving Info.:

Yields: 6 cups
Servings: 12
Serving Size: 1/2 cup
Points: 1-3 servings = 0 points
        4-7 servings = 1 point

*** Leave out the carrots and celery to make a Bolognese

Directions: *(for Ragu)*

1. Cook the onions, celery, carrots and garlic in a pot with olive oil cooking spray for 5-6 minutes, until they begin to sweat.
2. Add the broth. Cook for 5-10 minutes, or until almost all of the liquid has reduced.
3. Add the raw "italian sausage" ground turkey and cook till browned, breaking up the meat with a cooking spoon into small pieces.
4. Add the wine, vinegar, tomato paste, canned tomatoes, rosemary, allspice and italian seasoning. Bring to a boil.
5. Lower the heat and cook at low simmer, covered, for 30 minutes. Season to taste.

Buffalo Sauce

An addictively spicy hot sauce that holds the universe together

Serving Info.:

Yields: 1-1/2 cups
Servings: 6
Serving Size: 1/4 cup

Points:

1-2 servings = 0
3-6 servings = 1

Good old Buffalo sauce, a Holy Union between cayenne pepper-based hot sauce, vinegar and lots and lots and lots of butter. It's one of those things that everyone enjoys, but that most people trying to cut calories have to avoid because of the fat content. Well, that was true until the heavens opened, the clouds parted, choirs of angels started singing and I bestowed this virtually fat free gift upon you all. I make this sauce with Molly McButter fat free butter sprinkles, but I'll also include instructions for making it with I Can't Believe It's Not Butter Light butter spread, if you don't mind it being a little higher in points for more richness.

Ingredients:

- 3/4 cup water
- 2/3 cup Franks Red Hot Cayenne Pepper Sauce, Original
- 2 tsp worcestershire sauce
- 2 Tbsp white vinegar
- 3 tsp Molly McButter fat free butter flavored sprinkles
- 2 tsp cornstarch + a little water
- 1/8 tsp granulated garlic powder
- 1/4 tsp chicken flavored granules
      *(trust me, just roll with it)

Directions:

1 Combine the water, hot sauce, worcestershire sauce, vinegar, butter sprinkles, garlic powder and chicken granules in a small sauce pot.
2 Mix cornstarch with a little water to dissolve it, then pour it into the pot.
3 Bring the mixture to a boil over medium heat. Lower the heat and let the sauce continue at a low rolling boil for 4 minutes, stirring occasionally.
4. Remove from heat and place in a container or serving vessel.
5. Stir the sauce after 5 minutes to help prevent the top layer from getting a thick layer as it cools.

Note:

- Instead of Molly McButter, you can use actual butter spread for a richer flavor. Replace the Molly Mcbutter and 3/4 cups of water with 4 tablespoons of I Can't Believe It's Not Butter Light and 1/2 cup of water. This will give a much richer butter flavor but will increase the point value.

Butter Sauce Base

A WW-ified butter sauce that can be adjusted for any recipe

If there is one thing that you'd NEVER think you'd be having on Weight Watchers, chances are it's a low point butter sauce. C'mon, we're talking about using beautiful, golden, liquid fat, for goodness sake. However, as with most recipes in this guide/book, a little bit of messing with ingredient swaps, and a little trial and error, will work wonders for your cooking, as well as your waist line.

This butter sauce is a faaaaaantastic base for you to use as the foundation for a lot of sauces of your own making. You can add some herbs, wine, capers, a little reduced fat Parmesan, whatever you'd like. As it's written below, this sauce is very tasty, but it is tailor made for you to customize. Plug the recipe into your recipe builder and begin adding some fresh herbs (tip: some herbs cost a point after a certain amount), spices, and other seasonings. This sauce base is a game changer for trying to make a TON of low point traditional sauces.

Ingredients:

- 4 Tbsp I Can't Believe It's Not Butter - Light
- 1-3/4 cups water
- 3 tsp Molly McButter Butter Flavored Sprinkles
  (optional but **HIGHLY RECOMMENDED** for giving a lot more butter flavor with no added points)
- 1-1/2 tsp Chicken Flavored Bouillon
  (like is used to make instant broth)
- 3 tsp cornstarch, dissolved in a little water

Serving Info.:

Yields: 1-1/2 cups
Servings: 6
Serving Size: 1/4 cup

Points:

1 serving = 1 point
2 servings = 2 points
3 servings = 4 points

Directions:

1 Melt the butter spread in a small pot or sauce pan on medium heat.
2 Add the water, Molly Mcbutter and bouillon. Heat until just simmering.
3 Pour the dissolved cornstarch mixture into the pot and stir to combine.
4 Allow the sauce to simmer for 3-4 minutes, or until it thickens to your desired consistency.
5 Remove sauce from heat and pour into serving dish.

Note:

- If you do not want to use Molly McButter you can leave it out of the recipe. I would recommend using an extra 2 Tbsp of I can't believe it's not butter light in place of 2 Tbsp of water Adjust points accordingly

Cheese Sauce

A deliciously low point cheddar cheese base sauce

This page is devoted to all of you cheese heads out there. This is a very easy to make cheese sauce that is awesome on pretty much anything. It can be poured over a baked potato, tossed with pasta to make low point mac n cheese, the possibilities are pretty much endless. It's also extremely customizable and easy to dock up. The consistency of this sauce isn't thick and goopy like canned cheese sauce, it's a little thinner, like a traditional sauce.

Servings Info.:
Yields: 3 cups
Servings: 12
Serving Size: 1/4 cup

Points Value:
1 serving = 1 point
2 servings = 2 points
3 servings = 3 points

Ingredients:
- 2-1/4 cups water
- 1 can Campbell's Healthy Request Soup Condensed Cheddar Cheese Soup
- 1/2 tsp salt
- 1/2 tsp chicken flavored bouillon granules
- 1/8 tsp ground turmeric
- 2-1/2 Tbsp molly mcbutter fat free cheese sprinkles**
- 3-1/2 Tbsp cornstarch, mixed with a little water to dissolve

For Nacho Cheese Sauce add:
- 4oz can diced green chilis (mild, med., or hot)
- 1/4 tsp cayenne or chipotle chili powder

Directions:
1. In a medium sauce pot, combine the water, condensed soup, salt, bouillon, turmeric, and molly mcbutter cheese powder. Bring to a low boil over medium heat, whisking to combine the ingredients.
2. Mix the cornstarch with just enough water to dissolve, then pour into the simmering liquid, stirring to combine. Allow the mixture to continue at a low rolling boil for 5 minutes, whisking occasionally.
3. Turn off the stove and allow the mixture to cool for 5-10 minutes. The sauce will thicken slightly the more it cools.

Notes:
- If you cannot find Molly McButter Fat Free CHEESE sprinkles, most major grocery stores stock flavored seasoning powders near their popcorn in the snack aisle. *Kernel Season's* popcorn seasoning mixes sells a Nacho Cheddar powder. It is salty, so leave out the salt from the regular recipe. Enter it into the recipe builder to adjust points if you are using that powder.
- For Nacho Cheese sauce, use cayenne pepper for plain ol' heat. Adding chipotle chili powder (McCormick's) adds a little smokiness as well as heat.
- 1 can of the condensed soup shows as more points in the recipe builder. However, if you remove the soup from the can and do the points according to the weight of the ACTUAL contents of the can, it is lower in points, and how we get it to 1 point, from doing the points by weight.
- For an even thicker, really goopy Nacho Cheese sauce, you can add up to 1 additional tablespoon of cornstarch and still keep the first serving at 1 point.

Cilantro Lime Sauce

A simple and zesty sauce that packs some Latin attitude

This sauce is so simple and comes together so quickly that it'll come as a total surprise the first time that you make it. The flavorful mix of chicken broth, lime juice, garlic, and a bunch of fresh cilantro makes this an incredibly savory sauce. It punches you in the face with a nice bit of lime, followed by a strong flavor of cilantro. It pairs very well with Latin themed dishes, served over fish, chicken, beef and heck, even cardboard would taste great slathered in this stuff.

Though I'm using I Can't Believe It's Not Butter Light in this recipe, I give directions in the notes at the bottom of the page for how to make it a 0 point sauce with 1 simple ingredient substitution. Note that there is a **very important** issue with the points value that is mentioned at the bottom of the page.

Serving Info.:
YIELDS: 1-1/4 cups
Servings: 5
Serving Size: 1/4 cup

Point Values: *(See Notes)*
1 serving   = 0-1 point? **
2 servings = 1 point **
3 servings = 1 point **

Ingredients:
- 1 cup chicken broth
- 2 Tbsp water
- 5 second spray, Olive Oil cooking spray
- 3 Tbsp lime juice
- 2 medium cloves garlic, chopped
- 1 Tbsp I Can't Believe It's Not Butter Light
- 2-1/2 tsp cornstarch, dissolved with a little water
- 1 bunch fresh cilantro, finely chopped
- salt and pepper to taste

Directions:
1. Combine the chicken broth, water, lime juice, garlic, I Can't Believe It's Not Butter Light and cornstarch in a saucepan over medium heat. Spray into the sauce for 5 seconds with olive oil cooking spray and stir to blend all of the ingredients. Bring sauce to a low simmer.
2. Simmer the sauce for a few minutes to allow it to start thickening up a bit, then add all of the fresh chopped cilantro and stir to combine.
3. Simmer for 2-3 minutes to allow the sauce to tighten up a bit more. Remove from heat.

Notes:
- For a 0 point version of this sauce simply replace the 1 Tablespoon of I Can't Believe It's Not Butter Light with 3 teaspoons of molly mcbutter fat free butter sprinkles. The sauce will be 0 points in total.

- *POINTS DISCREPANCY*: When you enter this sauce into the recipe builder, by default it shows 1 serving as 1 point. However, when you scroll down to 0 servings then back up to to 1 serving... 1 serving stays at 0 points. It doesn't change to 1 point again until you get to the second serving. Then, if you scroll back to 1 serving again it goes back to 0 points. Have fun making sense of that. Feel free to decide for yourself if it's actually 0 points or 1 point for the first serving, because I have nooooo idea. The recipe builder is a little loopy like that with the points for a few of the sauces in here, once added into the builder. They show 1 point at first, then if you scroll to 0 servings and back to 1 serving they stay at 0.

Clam Sauce

A classic seafood sauce that's usually drenched in points

Servings:
- Yield: 4 cups
- Servings: 8
- Serving Size: 1/2 cup

Points:
1-2 servings = 1
3-4 servings = 2

Linguini with White Clam Sauce is one of those staples of traditional southern italian cooking. It's one of those dishes that we all love or have wanted to try, but we shy away from it because of how much wine and butter are typically in it. After a member on Connect requested that I take a look at WW-ifying it, I was able to come up with an ultra low point, low calorie, virtually fat free version that is light, delicious and extremely flavorful. Not to mention that it's 1 point for a REALISTIC portion size, not 2 points for 2 measely little Tablespoons of sauce like you'll find elsewhere. *mic drop*

Ingredients:
1/4 cup white wine, chardonnay
2-1/2 cups water
1/4 cup bottled clam juice
1 pinch red pepper flakes
3 tsp molly mcbutter butter sprinkles
5 garlic cloves, chopped (raw or roasted)
1 tsp chicken flavored bouillon granules
1 small onion, diced
2 (6oz) cans clams, chopped
2 Tbsp oregano, finely chopped
2 Tbsp parsley, finely chopped
2 Tbsp + 1 tsp cornstarch
olive oil cooking spray

Directions:
1 Add the wine, water, clam juice, pepper flakes, butter sprinkles, garlic, chicken granules and onion into a medium pot and heat to a low boil, simmer 3 minutes.
2 In a separate dish, mix the cornstarch with a little water to dissolve, then pour it into the pot of simmering liquid, stir to combine.
3 Lower the heat and let the sauce continue at a low rolling boil for 4 minutes, stirring occasionally.
4 Turn off the heat. Pour in the contents of the 2 cans of canned clams and their juices. toss in the chopped fresh herbs and finally, spray into the sauce 5 times with olive oil cooking spray. Season with salt and pepper, to taste.

Variation:
- Instead of butter sprinkles, you can use 3 tablespoons of I Can't Believe It's Not Butter Light, but adjust your points accordingly.
- Add 2 cups of canned, crushed or diced tomatoes and juices in place of 2 cups of water from the base recipe to create Clams and Tomato Sauce, a classic Neapolitan dish.

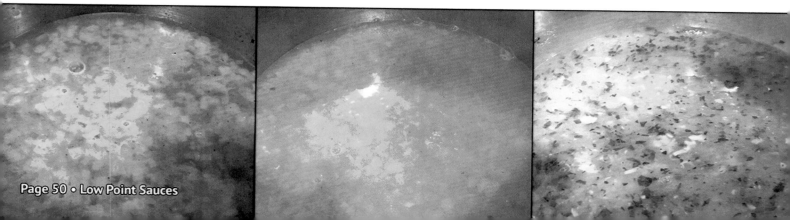

Sausage Country Gravy

Delicious flavor without the accompanying bypass surgery.

This WW-ified country gravy isn't a traditionally made gravy prepared by a grumpy line cook at a truck stop with a half pound of bacon grease... this is an incredibly low fat, low calorie version that still has a TON of flavor. Instead of full fat pork sausage, we are using a modified version of my 0 point breakfast sausage from page 15. Instead of heavy cream and a mountain of fat, we're going to be using unsweetened almond milk, and pan drippings, then pulling it all together with cornstarch and spices.

Serving Size:
Yields: 5 cups
Servings: (6) 3/4 cup

Points:
1 Serving = 1 points
2 Servings = 2 point

Ingredients:

Modified Breakfast Sausage:
- 1 pound extra lean ground turkey
- 1/2 tsp salt
- 1/4 tsp black pepper
- 1 tsp dried sage
- 1 tsp dried thyme
- 1 tsp fennel seed, ground (*I prefer ground fennel seed but you can use regular whole seeds*)
- 1 tsp onion powder
- 1/2 tsp dried marjoram
- 1/2 tsp smoked paprika
- 1/4 tsp maple extract (*optional for maple flavor*)
- 3 Tbsp fat free plain (or greek) yogurt
- 1/2 tsp red pepper flakes OR cayenne pepper (optional)

"City Boy" Country Gravy
- 1-1/4 cups unsweetened plain almond milk
- 3/4 cup plain fat free yogurt (creamier than greek)
- 1 cup water
- 1-1/2 Tbsp I Can't Believe It's Not Butter Light
- 4 Tbsp cornstarch
- 1/2 tsp salt
- Black pepper to taste, a bunch of it. (*I used around 1/2 tsp of fresh cracked black pepper, but season to your own taste.*)

NOTE:
- You can make the 1st serving 0 points by replacing the I Can't believe it's not butter light with 3tsp of Molly Mcbutter.

Directions:
1. Mix all of the sausage ingredients together in a mixing bowl. Cook in a LARGE pan or pot until the mixture is cooked through. Use cooking utensils to break up the meat during the entire cooking process to make sure it isn't just a bunch of big giant chunks o' turkey, finer is better.
2. In a mixing bowl, combine the almond milk, yogurt, water, I Can't Believe It's Not Butter, cornstarch, salt, and black pepper. Whisk to combine thoroughly.
3. Turn the pan up to high heat and give it a minute to get sizzling, stirring the meat so it doesn't burn.
4. Once the pan gets hotter than Ryan Gosling at your front door telling you "hey girl... I brought you one of dhallak's cupcakes, let me in." .... Pour the liquid mixture into the hot pan and start stirring. It should start to thicken up almost immediately.
5. Continue to stir on high heat, allowing the sauce to continue thickening for another minute or two, until it gets to a decent consistency.
6. Turn off heat and season with salt and pepper to your liking. A good amount of cracked black pepper gives a nice flavor to it.

Florentine Sauce

A delicously savory cream sauce loaded with fresh spinach

A Florentine Sauce is a savory cream sauce, loaded with fresh spinach, that is typically made with enough heavy cream and butter to give an adult grizzly bear a heart attack. This version is based on my lightened Bechamel sauce that you can find on page 42, primarily because it's a great flavorful creamy base... aaaaaand because I'm lazy, so there. This sauce goes well with poultry, fish, or served over eggs in Eggs Benedict, Eggs Florentine, or on top of an omelette.

Servings:

Yields: 4 cups
Servings: (6) 2/3 cup servings
Points: 1 point per serving

Ingredients:

3 cups prepared Bechamel Sauce, pg 42
3 medium garlic cloves, chopped
1 medium onion, diced
1/4 cup water**
1 tsp chicken flavored bouillon**
1 Tbsp white wine
3 tsp lemon juice
4 cups fresh spinach, packed
   (2) 12oz bags of spinach works.
Butter flavored cooking spray

Directions:

1 Cook the onions and garlic with butter flavored cooking spray for 1-2 minutes on medium heat, until onions begin to soften. Add the wine, bouillon, water, and lemon juice. Cook till liquid has evaporated.

2 Rough chop the spinach and then add it to the pan. Cover and cook until just starting to wilt.

3 Pour in the prepared Bechamel sauce, stir to combine, then cover pan with lid and simmer on low heat for 3-4 minutes.

4 Season with salt and pepper to taste

Notes:

1. Feel free to use frozen spinach if it is more convenient for you, though it may add more water to your sauce.
2. While making your Bechamel sauce, you can use 3 Tbsp of I Can't Believe It's Not Butter Light instead of Molly Mcbutter, but it will add 1 point.
3. You can replace the water and chicken bouillon with 1/4 cup of chicken broth and the sauce will stay 1 point per serving. **
4. Eating excessive amounts of spinach will **NOT** give you arms like Popeye or Mudhustler, regardless of what your mom told you as a kid.

Cook onions, garlic and spinach

Simmer with Bechamel

Use with Chicken, Seafood, and more

It's all Gravy Baby

This is honestly so simple that you're going to facepalm yourself

One of the most frequently requested sauces that I've been asked for that has always puzzled me, because honestly… it's really easy to make, is Gravy. Everyone always says that they miss gravy. I think it's because we're all so used to HAVING to make it 1 certain way, because "that's just how you make it." Get all of the fatty drippings from cooked meat, add a bunch of butter, or cream, or milk, with a garbage can full of flour used to thicken it. Why?!?! There's a really simple formula to make a low point gravy. Heat X amount of liquid, with Y amount of cornstarch, then you end up with Z amount of low point gravy.

Don't have pan drippings? Fine, use canned low sodium broth for your liquid. Don't have canned broth? Fine, use water and beef or chicken granules to make broth. Don't want to use cornstarch? Use Arrowroot. Mix it together, heat it up,… Done. There's a reason why saying that something is "Gravy" is saying that it's easy… it's because it's really easy to make low point.

Ingredients:

- 1-3/4 cups of "liquid." It can be pan drippings from meat that's prepared without any oil or butter, canned broth, water with bouillon, or any combination to make 1-3/4 cups of "Broth" that's no more than 1 point in total.
- 3 tsp cornstarch
- salt and pepper to taste

Directions:

1. Pour the 1-3/4 cups of "broth" into a small stock pot (strain the liquid if necessary to remove any solids from pan-drippings)
2. Mix the 3 teaspoons of cornstarch with a tiny bit of water to dissolve it. Pour the cornstarch mixture into the broth and stir.
3. Heat the mixture to a low boil, then reduce the heat and allow to simmer for 4-5 minutes, uncovered.
4. Remove from heat, season with salt and pepper, if needed, then pour into a dish and allow to cool for 5 minutes.

Serving Info.:
Yields: 1-2/3 cups
Servings: 6
Serving Size: 1/4 cup

Points:
1 serving = 0 points
2 servings = 1 point
3 servings = 1 point

Notes:
- You can substitute Arrowroot for cornstarch as a thickener. It may need to simmer a little longer.
- You can easily double or triple this recipe to make a big ol' barrel of gravy and as long as you follow the formula for liquid to cornstarch ratio, it'll work just fine.
- Remember, if you use drippings from meat cooked with a lot of oil and butter, it will change the points value of the gravy accordingly.
- In my gravy I had 3/4 cup of turkey drippings from my turkey, then added 1 cup chicken broth to get to my 1-3/4 cup.

Hollandaise Sauce

A luxuriously rich and creamy egg yolk and butter sauce

Hollandaise is pretty much the forbidden fruit of sauces when it comes to those of us trying to live a healthy lifestyle. Typically, we save up our points and calories to have the full fat version, or we buy prepackaged little tubes that cost a kidney. The traditional sauce is a very rich butter and egg yolk sauce, much like a warm mayonnaise. It's perfect over fish, vegetables and even potatoes. The most prized use for Hollandaise is, of course, Eggs Benedict, points be damned!

Luckily for all of your waistlines, I've come up with a way to drastically reduce the points that a GOOD SIZED serving of the sauce comes to, and by reduce the points, I mean that it's now 0 points. Under the current Freestyle guidelines, the only points in the sauce come from the enormous amount of butter in it. However, we can eliminate that completely and get the sauce to 0 points by using our good old friend Molly McButter (or *Butter Buds*), water and a little cornstarch as a complete 0 point replacement for the butter. So strap in folks and rejoice, heck, fill up a canteen with this sauce and cue the choirs of Angels to start singing.

Ingredients:

- 8 egg yolks (large eggs)
- 3 Tbsp white wine vinegar *(or lemon juice)*
- 1-1/4 cup water
- 16 whole black peppercorns
- 2 bay leaves
- 5 tsp molly mcbutter fat free butter sprinkles
- 1 tsp cornstarch, dissolved in a little water
- salt to taste
- pinch of paprika or cayenne pepper to garnish (optional)

Directions:

1. Heat the vinegar, 1 cup water, peppercorns, bay leaves and butter sprinkles to low boil. Simmer 3 minutes, turn off heat.
2. Allow mixture to cool for 20 minutes, then strain the liquid.
3. Whisk in cornstarch, egg yolks, remaining 1/4 cup of water and heat to a low simmer, stirring constantly as soon as the mixture begins to thicken.
4. Continue stirring on low heat, barely simmering for 5-7 minutes.
5. Turn off heat, season with salt to taste, if needed.
6. Pour sauce into serving dish or spoon over food. Garnish with a pinch of either paprika or cayenne. Sauce thickens as it cools.

Servings:

Yield: 1-1/2 cups
Servings: 3
Serving Size: 1/2 cup

Points:

1 serving = 0
2 servings = 1
3 servings = 1

NOTES:

- Everyone has EXTREMELY picky tastes when it comes to how they like their Hollandaise sauce. This recipe gives you a great low point foundation to add your own twist to make it taste more to your liking.
- If you do not have molly mcbutter, you can replace up to 1/2 cup of the water with an equal amount of I Can't Believe It's Not Butter Light spread, but that will take your sauce up to 4 points total. Using only 1/4 cup of ICBINB will keep your sauce at 0 points for the first serving, but the butter flavor will be barely noticeable.
- The sauce will thicken a little more as it cools due to the cornstarch. If it thickens too much, simply stir in water.

Low Point Hummus

Ok first thing's first... I know that Hummus isn't actually what you'd consider a sauce, but I don't care, it's awesome and I wanted to put it in because I have 2 versions of this yummy Middle Eastern dip. Traditionally, Hummus is made with garbanzo beans, garlic, lemon juice, tahini (crushed sesame seed paste), and lots and lots and looooooots of extra virgin olive oil. It's usually so high in points that the popular healthy cooking sites have their serving sizes at a mere 2 tablespoons to make it look low point, which anyone who has ever had hummus knows... that is NOT a realistic serving size.

People in Connect have been making and LOVING my original Low Point Hummus recipe for over half a year now. It gives you up to 1/2 cup of hummus for 1 point. I recently decided to also take a crack at making a low point chocolate hummus. Chocolate hummus is a sweet chocolaty dip that can be used for sliced fruit, dessert spreads, frosting pastries, or as an evil way to trick your kids into eating a bunch of pureed beans.

LOW POINT HUMMUS

YIELDS: 4 cups
Servings: 16
Serving Size: 1/4 cup
Points: 1-2 servings = 1 points

Ingredients:

- 29-30oz canned garbanzo beans/chickpeas, drained, reserve liquid
- 2 Tbsp tahini (sesame paste)
- 1/4 cup lemon juice
- 3-4 fresh garlic cloves (to taste)
- 2 Tbsp reserved garbanzo bean juice
- 3 Tbsp water
- 1/3 cup fat free yogurt (or greek)
- 1 tsp extra virgin olive oil
- 2 tsp ground cumin
- 1 tsp salt
- 1/4 tsp sesame oil *(OPTIONAL, though suggested)*

Directions:

- Drain the garbanzo beans, reserve the liquid, and rinse off the beans.
- Add the garbanzo beans, tahini, lemon juice, garlic, garbanzo bean juice, water, yogurt, oils, cumin, and salt to a large blender or food processor and process until pureed and smooth.
- If the mixture is too thick, add more reserved garbanzo bean juice, 1 Tablespoon at a time, until it takes on a very smooth, creamy, and easily spreadable consistency. Season with more salt and pepper, if necessary.
- Garnish with a dusting of paprika and minced parsley. Spray the top of the hummus with a quick touch of olive oil cooking spray.

CHOCOLATE "DESSERT" HUMMUS

YIELDS: 2-1/2 cups   POINTS: 1 serving = 0 points
Servings: 10   2-3 servings = 1 point
Serving Size: 1/4 cup   4-6 servings = 2 points

Ingredients:

- 30oz canned garbanzo beans/chickpeas, drained and thoroughly rinsed
- 6 Tbsp unsweetened vanilla almond milk
- 4 Tbsp unsweetened cocoa powder
- 8 tsp sugar free instant chocolate pudding mix
- pinch of salt
- 1 tsp caramel extract (or vanilla if you can't find it)
- 1-1/2 Tbsp sugar free maple syrup (pancake syrup)
- 1/4 cup 0 point sweetener (I used Monkfruit extract)
- 1/8 tsp ground cinnamon (OPTIONAL)
- 2 tsp powdered peanut butter (OPTIONAL)

Directions:

1 Add ALL of the ingredients into a food processor and puree on high for 1-2 minutes, or until mixture is completely smooth and creamy. Add a little bit more almond milk, if necessary.

NOTE:

- You can remove the peanut butter for allergy restrictions.
- I used monkfruit extract as my sweetener, but you can also use swerve, splenda, stevia or truvia. Monkfruit and Swerve seem to have no negative side effects for MOST people allergic to artificial sweeteners.
- You can leave out the cinnamon, or for an interesting twist, keep the cinnamon but also add additional cayenne chili powder for a mexican hot chocolate spiced hummus.
- This is so low in points that you can add some actual melted chocolate. Adjust your points. accordingly.

Marinara Sauce

A fast 0 point Marinara that's perfect for busy folks on the go

One of the first sauces that I ever put on connect is my "15 minute marinara." Is it an authentic little old Italian grandma recipe that calls for stewing imported tomatoes for 12 hours and using a gallon of red wine? Nope. Does it taste good, have depth of flavor, is 0 points and only takes 15-20 minutes to make from start to finish? Yes, yes and yes. This sauce is tailor made for busy folks on the go that want a sauce that tastes good, is quick and is also 0 points. The listed vegetables in the ingredients can be completely customized according to what you have in your fridge. Don't have bell peppers? Use a zucchini. Don't want to use carrots? Don't, use what you have. But having a mix of sauteed vegetables in the sauce will add great depth of flavor once pureed. It'll taste like you've been slaving over a stove for 5 days, like an old Sicilian grandma with four knees.

Ingredients:

- (2) 29-30oz cans of tomato sauce
- 1 medium onion, rough chopped
- 1 celery stalk, rough chopped
- 1 bell pepper, rough chopped, any color
- 1 Tbsp chopped garlic, or 4-5 fresh cloves
- 1 carrot, rough chopped
- 1/2 cup chicken broth
- 1 Tbsp italian seasoning
- 1/2 tsp paprika
- 1/2 tsp garlic powder
- 1/2 tsp onion powder
- 1/2 tsp dried basil
- 1 Tbsp red wine
- 1 Tbsp red wine vinegar
- 3 Tbsp stevia or sweetener of choice *(optional)*
- Red pepper flakes to taste *(optional)*
- Salt and Pepper to taste

Yield: 6-7 cups
Servings: 12-14 servings
Serving Size: 1/2 cup
Points: 0 points

Notes:

- You can use sugar instead of artifical sweetener, but you'll need to adjust points accordingly. By default, I usually use artifical sweeteners because I'm points crazy. Leave out the sweetener if you prefer your sauce to be more savory.
- Yes, there are pureed veggies in this, it's not a traditional tomato sauce. If you want to get all food snobby, go buy some 40 year old balamic vinegar and stew some tomatoes for 4 days. I'll be over here in the real world with kids.

Directions:

1. Cook all of the vegetables and garlic in a pot with olive oil cooking spray for 4-5 minutes on **high** heat until they begin to sweat. Add all of the seasonings and stir to mix over **high** heat for 3 minutes.
2. Add all of the other listed ingredients and cook on high heat till boiling. Lower the heat to medium and allow to simmer for 5 minutes, stirring occasionally.
3. Use an immersion blender or food processor to puree the sauce smooth, return to pot and season to taste.
4. Serve immediately or allow to sit longer so the flavors have more time to mingle. Playing soft jazz music and lowering the lights helps the seasonings to get it on.

Mexican Quick Molé

A simplified Quick Mole' sauce that can be thrown together in a pinch

Get ready to dodge angry mobs wielding torches and pitchforks because we're about to tackle the most holy of Mexican sauces, Mole' Poblano. Traditionally, Mole' is a very labor intensive sauce that takes an extremely long time to make and includes ingredients like bread, toasted nuts, seeds, peppers, oil, plaintains and much more. It usually cooks for hours or even days. This one is ultra fast, flavorful and only 1 points for a 1/2 cup serving.

Serving Size:
Yields: 6 cups
Serving Size: (12) 1/2 cup servings

Points Value:
1 servings = 1 point
2 servings = 3 points
3 servings = 4 points

Ingredients:

- 3 tsp sesame seeds, for toasting (toasted sesame seeds are less points)
- 4 tsp minced garlic (3-4 medium cloves)
- 29 oz canned tomato sauce
- 1/4 cup granulated stevia or sweetener of choice
- 1/4 cup unsweetened cocoa powder
- 1/2 tsp black pepper
- 3 Tbsp chili powder
- 2 tsp chipotle chili powder (optional but adds nice smokiness)
- 1-1/2 tsp ground cumin
- 1 tsp ground cinnamon
- 2 cups chicken broth, low sodium preferred
- 2 Tbsp PB2 or other brand powdered peanut butter
- 2 Tbsp masa harina (any corn flour will work)
- 1 tsp onion powder
- 3 Tbsp semi-sweet chocolate chips

Directions:

1. Toast the sesame seeds in a medium sized pot over medium heat for 2-3 minutes, till starting to brown, set aside to use as a garnish on your plated meal.
2. Spray pan with cooking spray and cook the garlic till just fragrant, don't burn it.
3. Add all of the other ingredients to the pot and bring to a boil. Lower the heat, cover and simmer for 15-20 minutes. Allow to cool for 30 minutes to let flavors meld. Garnish each serving with 1/4 tsp of toasted sesame seeds.

Note:
- If you do not want to use artificial sweeteners in your sauce, you can use regular sugar, which will raise the points value up to 2 points for 1 serving, 5 points for 2.

Pesto Sauce

A fresh, vibrant, savory & versatile green sauce

Pesto is an extremely delicious sauce, primarily consisting of finely processed garlic, tons of basil, different herbs and lots and lots and lots (did I say lots yet?) of olive oil. It is insanely yummie, but insanely high in points. Even popular "skinny" pesto recipes are typically a few points for a small 2 tablespoon serving size. We're upping our game by getting more olive oil flavor with some olive oil cooking spray, minimizing the amount of actual oil, and stretching it out with warm water.

Serving Size:

1/4 cup. (Makes 8 servings)

Points Value:

1 point per serving

Ingredients:

- 1 Tbsp pine nuts (to be toasted, lower points)
- 4 tsp minced garlic (3-4 medium cloves)
- 1 cup basil, packed, stems ok
- 3 cups spinach, packed
- 1/4 cup reduced fat grated parmesan cheese
- 1 cup warm water
- 2 tsp lemon juice
- 1 Tbsp extra virgin olive oil
- 1/2 tsp salt
- 1/4 tsp fresh ground pepper
- olive oil cooking spray, 5 second spray

Directions:

1 Heat a small sauce pan over medium-low heat for 1 minute, then add the pine nuts. Warm the pine nuts for 2-3 minutes, moving them, around the pan to toast them but avoid burning. Once they are toasted, remove from the pan and set aside.
2 Place all of the ingredients, including the pine nuts, into a food processor or large blender. Spray the olive oil cooking spray for 5 seconds directly onto the ingredients at close range to give them a fair amount of 0 point olive oil flavoring.
3 Process the mixture to break down all of the spinach and basil.

NOTE:

- Add more basil, spinach, arugala, or parsley to make a thicker pesto.
- You can substitute chopped walnuts in place of the pine nuts.

Piccata Sauce

Garlic, Lemon and Salty, Briny, Capery Awesomeness

In full disclosure, I understand that most of you reading this are thinking "What the heck is a caper?!" Yes, it COULD be a sneaky plan or bank heist, but it's also a tiny little ball of briny, salty goodness that looks kind of like a tiny sweet pea. I STRONGLY recommend that you buy and cook with **"Non Pareille"** capers. It's written on the jars, it just means those are small capers. Don't use the larger capers, as those are just a big salty jar full of yuck. You can find capers in the grocery store by the olives and vinegars typically.

Ingredients:

- 3/4 cup water
- 3/4 cup chicken broth
- 3 Tbsp lemon juice
- 2-3 cloves garlic, chopped
- 2 Tbsp capers
- 1 tsp dried parsley flakes
- 1-1/2 tsp cornstarch
- 1 Tbsp I Can't Believe It's Not Butter Light**
- Salt and pepper to taste
- 5 second spray, olive oil cooking spray
- Thin lemon slices for garnish
- Fresh chopped parsley for garnish

Serving Info.:

Yields: 1-1/2 cups
Servings: 4
Serving Size: 1/3 cup

Points Value:

1 point per serving

*** 0 points if you substitute 3tsp of molly mcbutter for the butter spread.*

Directions:

1 Sweat the garlic in a medium pan with olive oil cooking spray until it becomes fragrant, then add the water, chicken broth and I Can't Believe It's Not Butter to the pan. Heat to a simmer.
2 Stir in the lemon juice, parsley flakes and capers to the pan and return to a simmer.
3 Dissolve the cornstarch in a small cup with a tiny bit of water and then stir into the simmering sauce, it will begin to thicken immediately. Continue to stir for a few moments.
4 Allow the sauce to continue at a low simmer for a few minutes, until it thickens to the point where it can coat a spoon or rubber spatula.
5 Place the thin lemon slices into the simmering sauce and allow them to cook down slightly. Spoon the finished sauce over your meat. For best results, add your cooked meat to the pan and allow to simmer in the sauce for a minute, turning to coat.

Note: If you would like to make this sauce into a 0 point version, you can replace the I Can't Believe It's Not Butter Light with 3 teaspoons of Molly McButter Fat Free Butter Sprinkles. The flavor is unchanged.

Red Enchilada Sauce

This is a very fast, low fat and simple take on a Mexican classic

I need to start by addressing all of my Latino amigos that are reading this page. I understand that I've already messed with your Mole' sauce, I've already had you put fat free yogurt into Masa to make 3 point Gringo Tamales on Connect (#dhallakvids), I know that right now you're probably waving your fists in the sky and yelling "what more could this guy do to us?!" Well sorry, but I'm messing with your enchilada sauce now. Traditionally, red enchilada sauce is an incredibly delicious and spicy (depending on the peppers you use) puree of water, seasonings, a BOAT LOAD of oil and tons and tons and tons of dried hot chili peppers. In order to make it really low in points, we need to eliminate the oil. That's why I decided to replace it with tomato sauce and regular chili powder from the spice aisle. The reason being that it is more readily available to people and the thought of dealing with a big bag of dried chili peppers is an intimidating turn off to a lot of folks.

Ingredients:

- 2-1/2 cups water
- 1 tsp chicken flavored bouillon powder/granules
  (OR replace 1/2 cup of the water with 1/2 cup of chicken broth)
- 4 Tbsp california, chipotle, or anaheim chili powder
  (can use a different type of ground chili if desired)
- 1 Tbsp chili powder *(regular generic chili powder)*
- 1-1/2 tsp garlic powder
- 1-1/2 tsp onion powder
- 1-1/2 tsp ground cumin
- 1/4 tsp salt
- 30 oz canned tomato sauce *(0 point tomato sauce)*

Directions:

1 Pour ALL of the ingredients into a medium sized pot and stir to combine over medium heat.
2 Bring the sauce to a boil, then cover and reduce the heat to a low simmer. Allow sauce to simmer covered for 15 minutes, stirring occasionally.
3 Remove from heat and season to taste.

Serving Size:
Yields: 6 cups
Servings: (12) 1/2 cup

Points:
1 Serving = 0 points
2-4 Servings = 1 point
(up to 2 cups for 1 point)

NOTES:

1 Various types of dried chili powders can be found in the spice aisle or usually in the Latin section of most supermarkets.
2 Add actual pureed chilis or hot sauce if you want to add more 0 point heat.
3 Pairing this sauce with 1 point tortillas or wraps, 0 point seasoned meat, veggies, and the Fat Free cheese hack will give you extremely low point enchiladas.
4 This sauce goes really well with my 3 point Tamales, you can find them in Connect under *#dhallakvids*.

Roasted Red Pepper Marinara

A mildly sweet marinara-style sauce made with roasted red peppers

This sauce is proof that it may take me a long time to get to a recipe, but eventually I'll get around to it. About 5 months ago, I promised *@dtspilde* on Connect that I'd make a marinara sauce that doesn't have any tomato in it because of food allergies. After a little searching online, I found that making marinara sauce with Roasted Red Peppers is a great way to do it. The addition of red wine, chicken broth and the sauteed carrots and red onion also help give it more depth.

Ingredients:

- 5 large red bell peppers, chopped
- 5 medium cloves fresh garlic
- olive oil cooking spray
- 1 large red onion, rough chopped
- 1 cup chopped carrots
- 1 tsp italian seasoning
- 1/2 tsp garlic powder
- 1/2 tsp onion powder
- 1/2 tsp dried basil
- 1/2 tsp dried thyme
- 1 Tbsp I Can't Believe It's Not Butter Light
- 1-1/2 cups chicken broth
- 1/2 cup water
- 2 tsp red wine vinegar
- 2 Tbsp red wine

Serving Info.:

Yields: 5 cups
Serving Size: 1/2 cup
Servings: 10

Point Values:

1-2 servings = 0 points
3-7 servings = 1 point
8-10 servings = 2 points

Note:

- If you don't want to use red wine in your sauce, you can replace it with 2 Tbsp of Balsamic Vinegar for the same amount of points.
- Use this as a base for my red enchilada and mole' sauces, if you have tomato allergies.

Directions:

1 Preheat your oven to 425 degrees and line a sheet pan with aluminum foil, coat with olive oil cooking spray.
2 Cut the red peppers into large pieces, remove the seeds and arrange on the sheet pan along with the fresh cloves of garlic. Coat with olive oil cooking spray, season lightly with salt and pepper, then bake at 425 for 20 minutes, or until the peppers begin to blacken.
3 Spray a large saucepan with olive oil cooking spray and saute' the red onion and carrots for 2-3 minutes on medium-high heat. Add the I Can't Believe It's Not Butter Light and stir till it melts. Add the italian seasoning, garlic powder, onion powder, dried basil, thyme, water, vinegar, chicken broth and red wine. Bring to a low boil and allow to simmer for 3-4 minutes.
4 Pour the contents of the sauce pan into a food processor or large blender, along with all of the roasted garlic and red bell peppers.
5 Puree on high speed for a minimum of 1 minute or until the sauce is smooth, adding more water, as necessary to thin the sauce. Season with salt and pepper, to taste.

Roasted Tomatillo Sauce

A deliciously fresh and flavorful traditional Mexican green sauce

Ever been to a Mexican restaurant or taco shop and put that delicious green sauce on your food instead of the red stuff, or had enchiladas with green sauce? Maybe pork chili verde? Then you've had tomatillo sauce.

Traditionally, it's just a bunch of tomatillos, a type of fruit that resembles a firm green tomato with a papery husk, that are boiled and then thrown in a blender with some peppers and other stuff. What WE'RE going to do is add a lot more savory depth to it by roasting all of the vegetables until the skins start to blister and then process it.

Yield: 5 cups
Servings: 10 servings
Serving Size: 1/2 cup
Points: 0 points per serving

3 point chicken tamales with roasted tomatillo sauce

Ingredients:

- 2-1/2 lbs. Tomatillos, husks and stems removed
- 1 medium onion, rough chopped
- 2 medium green bell peppers, rough chopped, seeds removed
- 3 medium cloves garlic
- 4 good sized Pasilla peppers, chopped, seeds removed (they aren't spicy)
- 1/2 bunch fresh cilantro, around 1 handful
- 1/2 tsp salt
- 1 whole Jalapeno pepper *(OPTIONAL!)*

Notes:

- Tomatillos are very easy to clean for this sauce, just pull the husks back like the husks on an ear of corn, twist the stem and pull. Remove any dirt or debris and you're good to go.
- Tomatillos have a sticky feel to them, that's fine.
- Add the Jalapeno to the roasting pan, if you want a spicy sauce. This base recipe is for a completely mild and non spicy sauce.
- If you plan to use this sauce for enchiladas, add some water or chicken broth to thin it out a bit.
- This sauce is delicious served with tacos, tamales, over chicken, pork, on nachos, enchiladas, eggs, pretty much anything.

Directions:

1. Preheat your oven to 375 degrees.
2. Line a large sheet pan with foil and spray with olive oil cooking spray.
3. Place all of the vegetables on the tray and spray them liberally with the cooking spray, then sprinkle lightly with salt and pepper.
4. Cook the vegetables at 375 degrees for 45 minutes, or until the tops of the vegetables are starting to blacken.
5. Turn the broiler to high in your oven and place the tray on the top rack under the broiler. Watch so that the vegetables don't burn to a crisp. You want to develop some black char across the tops of some of them.
6. Remove the tray from the oven and spoon all of the roasted veggies into a food processor or large blender. Make sure to also pour all of the juices in as well, along with the fresh cilantro and 1/4 tsp salt.
7. Process the vegetables on high for up to 1 minute. It should give you a thick green salsa.

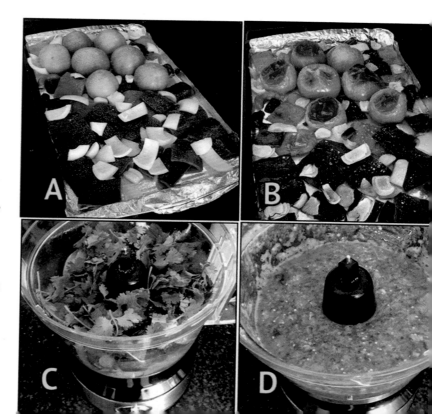

Satay Sauce

A deliciously creamy peanut butter, coconut, curry sauce

We know how amazing Thai Peanut Sauce is and we also know how full to the brim of pure fat the sauce is, as well. Typically made with a ton of whole fat coconut milk, full fat peanut butter and lots of sugar, Thai Peanut Sauce is a rare indulgence for most people trying to eat healthy. Or at least it was until the Low Point Ninja set his sights on it. This light version is incredibly easy to make and once you buy the ingredients, you'll be able to make a lot of it, after that initial purchase of some of the exotic ingredients.

Ingredients:

- 1-1/2 cup water
- 1 tsp asian chili sauce
- 1 tsp asian "fish sauce"
- 1 Tbsp reduced sodium soy sauce
- 1-1/2 tsp lime juice
- 1 Tbsp red curry paste
- 1/2 cup Coconut Milk Beverage, unsweetened
  (*"So Delicious!"* *"Silk"* and other brands of Almond Milk flavored coconut beverages)
- 6 tsp sweetener of choice (*splenda, stevia, truvia, monkfruit, swerve, etc.*)
- 11-1/2 Tbsp Powdered Peanut Butter (*that's 2/3 cup + 1-1/2 Tbsp*)
- 4-1/2 tsp cornstarch

Serving Info.:

Yields: 2 cups
Servings: 8
Serving Size: 1/4 cups

Points Value:

1 serving = 1 point
2 servings = 3 points
3 servings = 4 points

Directions:

1. Combine the chili sauce, soy sauce, lime juice, curry paste, water and fish sauce in a medium sized pot. Stir to combine and begin heating over medium heat.
2. In a separate mixing bowl, add the coconut milk beverage, powdered peanut butter, cornstarch and sweetener. Whisk to combine till no lumps remain.
3. Pour the coconut milk mixture into the pot with the curry water and heat to a simmer. Turn down the heat and allow the sauce to continue at a low rolling boil for 5 minutes, stirring so that the peanut butter doesn't stick to the bottom of the pan.
4. Remove from heat and pour the mixture into a large bowl, dish, or other vessel to cool for 15-20 minutes, it will thicken as it cools.
5. Stir the mixture **EVERY 5 MINUTES** to avoid having the top of the sauce become a thick solid film as it cools. After 15-20 minutes of cooling and stirring, the sauce is done and should remain creamy, thick and smooth without the top firming up.

Note: If you cannot find "So Delicious" or "Silk" brand coconut beverage, try to find a coconut flavored beverage, even almond milk based, that scans for 1 point for 1/2 cup serving. You can also try regular almond milk with 1 teaspoon of coconut extract.

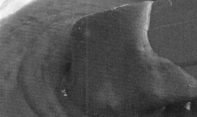

Scampi Sauce

A spicy, lemon butter, white wine, garlic, herb sauce

Scampi sauce is a delicious, zesty, herbed lemon garlic sauce that goes fantastic with all types of seafood and poultry. It's most popular application is, of course, Shrimp Scampi. In this recipe I'll be adding Shrimp into the ingredients, even though this is really supposed to be a recipe page for just the sauce. I'm including how to actually use it to make a dish,.. why not, it's my book after all. There two things to note in this recipe: (1) If you don't want to use Molly Mcbutter, you can definitely use 2-3 Tbsp of I Can't Believe It's Not Butter Light, and, (2) Your sauce will go up to 1 point. All of the ingredients in the sauce are measured to be at 0 points, however, the moment you add 1 Tbsp of Oregano, it takes the sauce to 1 point. Ignore that.

Ingredients:

- 3 tsp chopped garlic, 3-4 medium cloves
- 5 second spray, olive oil cooking spray
- 1-1/4 cup water
- 1 Tbsp white wine
- 2 tsp white wine vinegar
- 1 tsp cornstarch + a little water to dissolve
- 3 tsp molly mcbutter fat free butter sprinkles
- 1 Tbsp lemon juice
- 1 tsp chicken flavored bouillon powder (I use Knorr brand)
- 1/8 tsp black pepper
- 1/8 - 1/4 tsp red pepper flakes to taste *(OPTIONAL)*
- 1 Tbsp finely chopped fresh parsley, packed
- 1 Tbsp finely chopped fresh oregano, packed
- 1-1/2 to 2 pounds cleaned and deveined shrimp or diced chicken breast

Servings:

Yields: 1 cup sauce
Servings: 4
Servin Size: 1/4 cup sauce

POINTS:

Points: 0 points per serving **

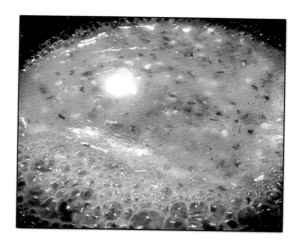

Directions:

1. Spray a medium saucepan for 5 seconds with olive oil cooking spray, then saute garlic over medium heat till fragrant.

** Note: The recipe builder will increase the sauce to 1 point once you add fresh oregano into the recipe. IGNORE IT!!! It's 1 tbsp of 0 point herb.

2. Add all other ingredients EXCEPT the shrimp and herbs, to the pan and bring to a simmer. Once the sauce begins to thicken, add the fresh herbs and stir.

3. Add the cleaned shrimp or diced chicken to the sauce and simmer for 4-5 minutes or until the shrimp starts to turn pink (or your chicken is cooked through). Remove from heat and serve alone, over rice or with pasta.

White Wine Butter & Garlic Sauce

A delicious herbed garlic butter sauce with a subtle wine taste

Servings Info.:

- Yields: 1-3/4 cups
- Servings: 7
- Serving Size: 1/4 cup

Points:

1 serving = 1 point
2 servings = 2 points
3 servings = 3 points

You would be a straight up liar if you said that you didn't love a good white wine butter sauce, but let's see... what's the main problem with that sauce if you're in Weight Watchers® ? Oh yeah, a giganto amount of points from butter and wine. Here's the deal though, simply follow the ideas in this guide and figure out how to OUT SMART your food. A few simple food swaps from thinking outside of the box makes this sauce possible. We up the servings by stretching it out with water and chicken broth to lower the points per serving. Ask yourself, do we REALLY need 1/2 cup of white wine in the sauce? Guess what, 1/4 cup of it still gives a nice wine flavor for less points. Do we really need a ton of butter? Nope. Let's use I Can't Believe It's Not Butter Light instead to impart a buttery flavor at a fraction of the points. What we end up with is an extremely low fat, low calorie wine sauce.

Ingredients:

- 1/2 cup chicken broth
- 1 cup water
- 1/4 cup white wine (I used chardonnay)
- 1 tsp minced garlic (1 medium clove)
- 2 Tbsp I Can't Believe It's Not Butter Light
- 1 tsp dried parsley flakes
- 2-1/2 tsp cornstarch
- salt and pepper to taste

Directions:

1 Combine all of the ingredients in a small sauce pot, whisk to combine.
2 Bring the sauce to a low boil over medium heat.
3 Allow the sauce to continue at a low boil for 2-3 minutes, whisking occasionally while the sauce continues to thicken a bit.
4 Remove from heat and season with salt and pepper, to taste.

Notes:

- If you would like a creamier sauce for no additional points, you can replace 1/4 cup of the water with 1/4 cup of unsweetened almond milk. You can also use 3 Tbsp of fat free/skim milk in place of an equal amount of the water.
- You can add in some red pepper flakes, different herbs than parsley, and some lemon juice, but then you'd be treading on the "Scampi Sauce" recipe's territory.
- Don't want to use wine? Substitute the white wine with 2 Tbsp of white wine vinegar.

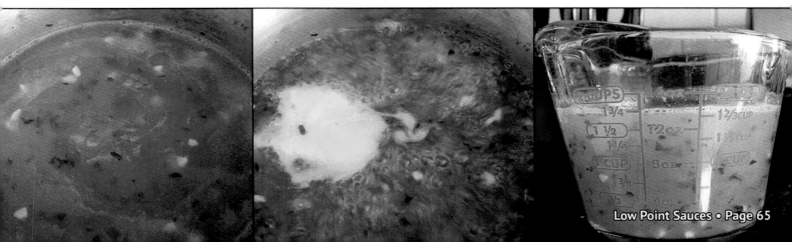

HOLIDAY SIDES

My special gift to you this Holiday season, a buuuunch of traditional low point sides

Once again I have to give a special thanks to @andmatsmom from Connect for convincing me to do this. She contacted me in September and said that she felt it would be a good idea if I were to try and make a bunch of low point Thanksgiving side dishes to help everyone out this year. In typical male fashion I whined, dragged my feet and said "I don't want to." (insert pouty faced emoji). Like all things in this world, if we men would just shut our yaps and listen to the ladies, the world would be a better place.

The tsunami of thanks and praise that I received from putting these together, completely and utterly blew me away. I wasn't expecting it in the least. In the lead up to Thanksgiving, there were so many people in Connect that were stressing and filled with anxiety about what they could make that wouldn't sabotage all of their progress. As soon as I started rolling these recipes out, the amount of thanks, praise, and over the top happiness from everyone completely caught me off guard. What was even more special was all of the posts that I started getting tagged in. People thanking me and showing me pictures and videos of their family enjoying the dishes, heartfelt posts from people saying how happy they were, how delicious the meals were and how they were able to enjoy Thanksgiving without worry. There was absolutely no way that I could have this cooking guide without including these as well.

".. on the day of Thanksgiving dhallak
delivered unto the people 2 point stuffing
and 1 point corn muffins, and it was good..."
- The Book of Freestyle 12:7

Side Dishes

This is a small list of Holiday themed sides that I was racing to try and get finished before this past Thanksgiving. Hopefully, these will be able to help more of you this Christmas as well.

Mashed Cauliflower

Pureed cauliflower loaded with roasted garlic and fresh rosemary

Servings:
Yield: 2.5 cups
Servings: 4
Serving Size: 2/3 cup

Points:
1 serving = 0 points
2-4 servings = 1 point

I know that potatoes versus cauliflower is a heated debate that invoked fury and anger amongst opposite sides of the aisle, but c'mon folks... I'm the low point guy, what did you think you were going to get from me? This recipe makes a smooth and creamy savory cauliflower puree that has a texture that is comparable to creamy mashed potatoes. Does it taste exactly like them? Of course not... it's cauliflower! But it tastes great and is a good low point substitution if you're watching points or carbs.

Ingredients:
- 2 lbs cauliflower florets
  - thawed if frozen
- 1 medium onion, chopped
- 1 Tbsp I Can't Believe It's Not Butter Light
- 4-5 medium cloves roasted garlic
  (pg. 33 of my download)
- 1 Tbsp packed fresh rosemary, chopped
- 1/2 tsp onion powder
- 1/4 tsp garlic powder
- 1/2 tsp chicken bouillon
- 3 Tbsp plain fat free yogurt (or Greek)
- 2 Tbsp chicken broth
  (plus more if needed)**
- butter flavored cooking spray (optional)
- salt and pepper to taste

Directions:
1. Spray a large saucepan or stock pot with butter flavored cooking spray. Add the butter spread and onions, cook until the onions soften.
2. Add the cauliflower florets, roasted garlic, rosemary, onion powder, garlic powder, chicken bouillon and chicken broth into the pan and cover. Reduce heat to med.-low and cook for 15 minutes or until cauliflower is soft, stirring occasionally.
3. Turn off heat. Spoon the contents of the pan into a food processor. Add the yogurt and a dash of salt and pepper. Process the cauliflower on high speed until smooth, it could take 2-3 minutes. Add more chicken broth, a little at a time, if the mixture is too thick. Be careful, as you don't want to add too much liquid all at once and make the puree too thin. You're aiming for mashed potato consistency.
4. Return the puree to a large pot for holding, or into a large serving vessel. Season with salt and pepper if needed.

Notes:
- If you would like to use regular garlic instead of roasted, use 1 Tbsp. of chopped fresh garlic. Add it in with the cauliflower florets during the cooking process.
- If you add too much broth and make the puree too thin, you can thicken it with instant mashed potato flakes. Add them 1 Tbsp at a time to the hot puree in the food processor and process until smooth. Add more as necessary. Adjust points accordingly.

Corn Muffins

Getting "REAL" cornbread down to 1 point. BOOMshakalaa!!!

Alright folks, I had a LOT of requests to include my cornbread muffin recipe into this Thanksgiving download because, well... cornbread. One of the first things I made when I started Weight Watchers was an old school cornbread recipe that's been floating around in-program for decades. Pretty much just cornmeal, egg, and a can of creamed corn. For the life of me, I couldn't figure out WHY they had to be 2 points each, there HAD to be a smarter way to do it. All it took was a little bit of alone time with the recipe builder, a glass of wine, some Marvin Gaye... and 9 months later we have 1 point cornbread. Seriously though... instead of the creamed corn, which has points, blend up a can of 0 point corn with a bit of sweetener. Boom, goodbye 11 points. Then I saw that corn flour has slightly less points than cornmeal So, by using a mix of corn flour AND cornmeal we're able to drop these babies down to 1 point each for the first 2 muffins. What's the moral of the story? Get creative in the recipe builder.

Ingredients:

- 1-1/4 cups masa harina (corn flour)
- 3/4 cup yellow cornmeal
- 3 tsp baking powder
- 3 large eggs
- 1 tsp salt
- 2 Tbsp sweetener (monkfruit, swerve, splenda, etc)**
- (2) 15oz cans whole kernel corn with their liquid
  - Scan it to make sure you pick 0 point cans of corn. Scan Scan Scan.
- 1/2 cup whole corn kernels, frozen, canned & drained, it doesn't matter, just make sure they are 0.
- 1 Tbsp of skim milk or almond milk

Directions:

1. Preheat oven to 400 degrees.
2. Line cupcake/muffin tins with liners. I personally like to use foil liners because I am cursed. Any time that I use the paper liners, EVERYTHING always sticks to them. Yes, even with spray. I hate paper liners. I only used them in the pic up top because I was out of foil ones. Paper liners = evil.
3. Put the corn flour and yellow cornmeal into a large mixing bowl, along with the baking powder, salt and sweetener. Stir to combine.
4. Beat the 3 large eggs in a mixing bowl until they are crying and hand over their lunch money. Set aside.
5. Put the entire contents of the 2 cans of 0 point corn, as well as the sweetener (or sugar) and milk into a blender, food processor, or use an immersion blender to roughly blend the corn together with the liquid into a rough chopped corny slurry. Congrats, you've just replaced high point canned corn with an all natural substitution that's 0 points. Booyah.

Servings Info.:

Yield: 24 muffins
Servings: Umm... 24. 🤪
Serving Size: 1 muffin

Point Values: **

1 serving = 1 points
2 servings = 2 points
3 servings = 4 points

6. Pour the blended corn mixture into the bowl with the dry ingredients, along with 1/2 cup of whole corn kernels and the beaten eggs that are probably still crying. Mix it all together until well combined. Set aside and let sit for 10 minutes.
7. Fill the cupcake liners 3/4 full with the batter that has fluffed up a little bit over the time it was resting.
8. Bake at 400 degrees for 14-18 minutes. Mine took 16.

NOTES:

- YES, THESE ARE REGULAR SIZED! There is a special place in the lake of fire for people who give out muffin and cupcake recipes that are for MINI baked goods and don't tell you they are. Then you get your hopes all up and are all "hurray, cupcakes!" Then you make them and are all sad like when you found out about Santa and the Easter Bunny.
- If you are using a shiny, thin cupcake pan, they seem to take longer to cook than if you are using a darker, thick nonstick cupcake or muffin pan.
- You can substitute the 2 Tbsp of sweetener for 2 Tbsp of regular sugar if you'd like, but the points will change to 1 point for 1 muffin, 3 points for 2 muffins and 4 points for 3 muffins.
- People in Connect have been making batches of these muffins and using them to make cornbread stuffing with a modified version of my stuffing recipe.

Green Bean Casserole

We're putting a lighter spin on a classic side dish

Green bean casserole is a holiday staple that's usually pretty high in points. We're making it lower in points by adding mushrooms and onions to stretch out the number of servings, which will decrease the points per serving. We're also using reduced fat grated parmesan as a low point tasty binder.

Servings Info.:

Yield: 7 cups
Servings: 13
Serving Size: 2/3 cup

Point Values:

1 serving = 2 points
2 servings = 4 points
3 servings = 6 points

Ingredients:

- 1 large onion, chopped
- 3 cloves fresh garlic, chopped
- 16 oz. fresh sliced mushrooms
- 1/2 cup chicken broth
- 2 tsp worcestershire sauce
- 1 tsp onion powder
- 1/2 tsp garlic powder
- 2 (10.5 oz) cans reduced fat/sodium condensed cream of mushroom soup (see note)**
- 2 tsp cornstarch, dissolved in a little water
- 9 cups frozen cut green beans, thawed (*3 12 oz bags*)**
- 1/4 cup grated parmesan topping, reduced fat
- 1 cup French's crispy fried onions, crushed and packed
- salt and pepper to taste

Directions:

1. Preheat oven to 350 degrees, then spray a large pan with cooking spray and cook onions and garlic on medium heat, 4-5 minutes until softened.

2. Add chicken broth, onion powder and garlic powder to the pan, cover and cook for 5 minutes at a low simmer.

3. Add the sliced mushrooms to the pan, cover, and cook for 5 minutes over medium heat.

4. Stir in the 2 cans of cream of mushroom soup and dissolved cornstarch. Stir until well combined and contents of the pan are coated.

5. Cook at a low simmer uncovered for 5 minutes, stirring occasionally. Season with salt and pepper.

6. Remove pan from heat. Add all of the green beans to the pan and gently fold to combine. Coat all of the beans with the sauce. Return to heat until just heated through.

7. Once the sauce has started to bubble, turn off the heat and stir in the grated parmesan cheese and 1/4 cup of crushed French's fried onions.

8. Pour the contents of the pan into a 3 quart casserole dish. Bake for 40 minutes at 350.

9. Remove pan from oven and sprinkle top of the casserole with 3/4 cups of crushed French's fried onions. Return the casserole to the oven, turn the oven temperature up to 375 degrees and cook for an additional 10-15 minutes.

10. Allow the casserole to cool uncovered for 10 minutes before serving. Sauce thickens more as it cools.

NOTES:

A) You can use fresh cut green beans instead of the frozen ones, in which case I would recommend either boiling them in water for a few minutes to soften them a little bit and then rinse them under cold water to stop the cooking process, or sautee them covered for 4-5 minutes and then remove from heat and set aside. Then follow the directions as normal.

B) If you don't want to use mushrooms, you can replace them with more green beans. You need to make up the bulk of the removed mushrooms with something else to keep the same number of servings and points.

C) You can replace the low fat/sodium condensed cream of mushroom soup, with cream of chicken soup if you don't like mushrooms.

D) If your sauce is TOO thick at the end of step 5, stir in a little bit more chicken broth to thin it.

E) Don't forget to taste the sauce prior to mixing in the green beans so that you can add more seasoning, if needed.

F) One of the BIGGEST things that you might be trying to figure out is the how I came up with 9 points for 2 (10.5 oz) cans of reduced fat/sodium cream of mushroom soup, rather than the 12 points that the WW app would lead you to think it is. Well, allow me to explain, because the actual soup can is wrong in this case. The CAN of soup says that 1 serving size is 1/2 cup and that there is 2.5 servings (1.25 cups per can). HOWEVER.... the can is wrong. If you actually pour the contents of the can out and measure them there is exactly 1 cup of condensed soup per can, not 1-1/4 cups like the can's listed servings (and points) suggest.

If you enter the nutritional info for the can into the app with 2 servings (1 cup) rather than 2.5 servings (1.25 cups), it gives a point value of 4 points for 1 cup (the real contents of the can, not 1.25 cups). The contents of 2 cans of soup, which is 2 cups, is 9 points. This is a BIG difference from the points that would show from just scanning the can. It isn't the WW database's fault. The can lists 1.25 cups of contents, when it really only has 1 cup.

Dressing / Stuffing

Tackle this turkey day hurdle with a few very smart ingredients swaps

With the holidays fast approaching, I wanted to do what I could to try and offer help, so that you CAN have a delicious and low point holiday meal, INCLUDING dressing/stuffing. You'd think that there's no way to possibly have low point dressing that doesn't taste like cardboard, but it's totally doable. You just have to be smart about it. Glance at the recipe and you'll see that all we really had to do was use low point bread. I also removed the butter. We're getting a buttery flavor by cooking with butter flavored cooking spray.

Servings Info.:

Yield: (1) 3 qt. Casserole Dish
Servings: 12
Serving Size: 3/4 cup

Point Values:

1 serving = 2 points
2 servings = 3 points
3 servings = 5 points

Ingredients:

* 16 slices Sara Lee 45 Calorie Bread
  (or other brand 1 point/slice sandwich bread)
* 2 cups onion, diced
* 2 cups celery, diced
* 1-1/2 cups carrot, diced
* 3 cups chicken broth
* 2 large eggs
* 2 medium garlic cloves, chopped
* 2 Tbsp fresh rosemary, finely chopped
* 2 Tbsp fresh sage, finely chopped
* 2 Tbsp fresh thyme, finely chopped
* 1 tsp onion powder
* 1 tsp garlic powder
* salt and pepper to taste

Ground Turkey:

* 1/2 lb. 99% fat free ground turkey
* 1 tsp worcestershire sauce
* 1/2 tsp paprika
* 1/2 tsp onion powder
* 1/2 tsp garlic powder
* 1/2 tsp ground cumin
* 1/4 tsp each salt and pepper
* 1 Tbsp plain fat free or greek yogurt

Directions:

1. Preheat oven to 250 degrees. Cut sliced bread into 1/2 inch cubes and spread onto baking sheet. Bake for 25-40 minutes, or until the bread is completely dried out, but not burned. Look in every 10 minutes after 25 minutes to check. Set aside.

2. Mix all of the ingredients for the turkey portion of the recipe in a mixing bowl until well combined. Heat a large sauce pan over medium-high heat. Spray the pan with butter flavored cooking spray and cook the meat until just cooked through. Use a kitchen utensil to break up the meat into smaller pieces during cooking. Remove from pan, set aside.

3. Dice the onions, celery, carrots, garlic and set aside. Finely chop fresh rosemary, sage and thyme.

4. Spray the pan that you cooked the ground turkey in with butter flavored cooking spray. Cook the onions, carrots, celery and garlic over medium heat for 5-6 minutes, until they begin to soften.

5. Add the chicken broth and fresh herbs to the pan, along with the garlic powder and onion powder. Cook at a low simmer for 15 minutes. Turn off the heat, stir in the turkey, season with salt and pepper. Cool for 10-15 minutes.

6. Whip the 2 large eggs and stir them into the cooled pan of vegetables and broth. Place all of the dried bread in a large mixing bowl, pour the vegetable/broth mixture over the bread and mix to combine. Add more broth if the mixture is too dry, though it should be ok.

7. Preheat oven to 325 degrees. Pour the dressing mixture into a 3 quart (13"x9") casserole dish sprayed with butter flavored cooking spray. Gently spread the mixture out evenly. Cover the casserole dish with aluminum foil and bake for 25 minutes. After 25 minutes, take the dish out of the oven, remove the foil, and use a kitchen utensil to gently "fluff" the dressing up without breaking it apart. Return the casserole to the oven and bake uncovered for an additional 15 minutes. Done.

NOTES:
A) The store near my house only has Sara Lee 45 calorie WHOLE WHEAT bread, that's what I used. Even though it was whole wheat bread, it was still very, very tasty. There are a few different brands of sliced bread out there that are 1 point per slice. If you can't find one, then most major supermarkets (around here anyways) carry "Nature's Own" Butter Bread, which is 3 points for 2 slices. Good luck, there's low point bread out there.
B) You can stretch this even further by adding some mushrooms to the veggies, or diced apples.
C) Feel free to swap out the ground turkey for oysters or any other protein that you want. The meat gives a different texture from the mushy dressing and soft veggies, plus it stretches out an extra serving. You can add the full 1 pound if you want, just up the garlic and onion powders and the cumin.
D) Add more broth if you want your dressing to be a little mushier. It's totally your call on how you like your dressing.
E) You can also choose to bake the stuffing in individual cupcake size portions. Just scoop 3/4 cup servings into cupcake pans, cover with foil so that the dressing doesn't dry out, then baking at 325 for 20-25 minutes.
F) You can also make a modified version of this dressing using my corn muffins instead of bread to make cornbread stuffing.
G) You can let your cubed bread air dry ahead of time, rather than baking it in the oven to dry it out.

Sweet Potato Casserole 2.0

An awesome and low point twist on a Thanksgiving classic

In order to get this baby down in points, we need to think of how to stretch out the points from the sweet potatoes, while still keeping the integrity of the dish and a good flavor profile. To accomplish this, we've cut the sweet potato with a larger amount of 0 point items that complement it. Namely, we've created a delicious mash of roasted sweet potato, butternut squash, carrot and canned pumpkin puree. Now that's using your noodle, folks.

Servings Info.:

Yield: 9 cups
Servings: 12
Serving Size: 3/4 cup

Point Values:

1 serving = 3 points
2 servings = 6 points
3 servings = 9 points

Ingredients:

- 1 pound Sweet Potato/Yam, slice in half horizontally
- 1 pound carrots, peeled (I used baby carrots for ease)
- 12 cups butternut squash, peeled and cubed. Around 4 pounds will give you 12 cups.
- 30 oz. canned pumpkin puree (0 point cans)
- 1/2 cup pecans, chopped and crushed to fit as much as you can into that 1/2 cup.
- 2 tsp ground cinnamon, divided
- 1-1/2 tsp pumpkin pie spice
- 2 tsp sugar
- 1 tsp maple extract (can be found in the spice aisle by the vanilla extract)
- 7 Tbsp sugar free maple syrup (pancake syrup)
- 2 slices turkey bacon, cooked, allowed to dry, then broken into small crumbled pieces
- 3/4 cup mini marshmallows, packed
- butter flavored cooking spray
- salt and pepper
- 2 large eggs

Directions:

1. Preheat oven to 400 degrees. Line 2 or 3 large baking sheet pans with parchment paper or foil and spray with cooking spray. Put the carrots, butternut squash and sweet potatoes into large mixing bowls (there's a lot of them). Spray to coat with butter flavored cooking spray, mix and spray to coat completely. Arrange the vegetables on the prepared sheet pans.

2. Place the veggies and squash into the oven and roast for 30 minutes at 350 degrees.

3. Remove the pans from the oven and put the carrots and butternut squash into a large container and set aside. Return the sweet potato halves to the oven and bake for an additional 15-20 minutes until soft. Remove from oven and set aside.

4. While the veggies are roasting, you'll prepare the candied pecans. Heat the pecans in a sauce pan without any butter or cooking spray on medium heat for 4-5 minutes, stirring to ensure they don't burn. When they start to get fragrant and darken in color slightly, stir in 1 tsp sugar and 1/2 tsp of cinnamon, stir to combine. Add 1 Tbsp of water and 1 Tbsp of sugar free syrup, stir until the liquid dissolves. Remove from heat and set aside in bowl.

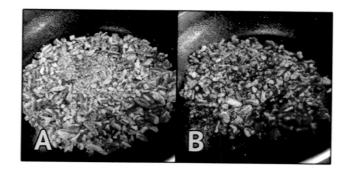

A   B

5. Heat the pumpkin puree in a pot over medium-low heat to just warm it. Add the maple extract and all of the remaining cinnamon, pumpkin pie spice and sugar free maple syrup. Stir to mix.

6. Place the roasted squash, carrots and sweet potato into a food processor in batches and blend on high speed until processed to ALMOST a smooth puree. You want to keep some texture to it. Scoop out each batch into a large mixing bowl.

7. Add the pumpkin puree to the large mixing bowl and use a rubber spatula to fold all of the pureed vegetables and pumpkin together. Add the eggs and mix to combine.

8. Spray a large 3 quart (9"x13") casserole dish with butter flavored cooking spray, then spoon all of the mash into the dish and spread evenly.

9. Spread the mini marshmallows along the top of the sweet potato mixture, then sprinkle the toasted pecans and crushed bacon bits. Drizzle the final 2 Tbsp of sugar free syrup around the casserole.

10. Bake the casserole for 15-20 minutes at 375 degrees, or until the marshmallows are slightly brown and toasted. Remove from oven. Enjoy.

NOTES & SUGGESTIONS:

- I would ONLY recommend using the marshmallows on this if you plan to serve it within 1-1.5 hours of making it. I noticed that around 2 hours after baking that the marshmallows were starting to "deflate", and at the 3 hour mark, they were flat and in desperate need of some Viagra
- If you don't want to use marshmallows on your casserole, you can leave them off and have an extra 6 ingredient points to play with. That would allow you to add an additional 1/4 cup of candied pecans to the topping instead.
- If you would like your casserole to be a little sweeter, you can add an additional 4 teaspoons of sugar into the pumpkin puree and the total point value will still JUST barely be 3 point for the first serving, but the second serving will be 7 points. It's up to you.
- Feel free to use regular maple syrup instead of sugar free syrup, but doing so will raise the point value up to 5 points per serving.
- If you don't mind artificial sweeteners, feel free to sweeten the bajeesus out of this baby.

Cheesy Gnocchi Casserole

Ricotta & Parmesan pasta dumplings that'll kick yo momma's Mac n Cheese to the curb

This is a low point and crazy-elevated take on a mac n' cheese casserole. Rather than using ultra high point store bought pasta, we're making our OWN fresh pasta dumplings. Don't be scared. If you can make 2 ingredient dough, YOU can make fresh pasta. By stretching it out with 0 point ingredients, we increase the servings and decrease the total points per serving. Outsmart your food, folks. There is no reason you can't eat like royalty for under 4 points. This recipe has a lot of steps, but you can totally do this.

Ingredients:

--- 0 Point AWESOME Italian Sausage:

- 1 lb. 99% fat free ground turkey
- 1 tsp ground fennel seed
  *I buy whole seeds and put them in a cheap $8 coffee grinder from ebay. Though you can use whole seeds if you have to, but ground is better.
- 1/2 tsp garlic powder
- 1/2 tsp onion powder
- 1/2 tsp dried basil
- 1 Tbsp dried parsley flakes
- 1 tsp dried italian herb seasoning
- 1 Tbsp chicken or beef granules/bouillon
  - it's the powdered stuff to make instant broth
- 3/4 tsp paprika
- 1/4 tsp salt
- 1/4 tsp pepper
- 2 Tbsp red wine vinegar
- 3 Tbsp fat free greek yogurt (trust me)
- red pepper flakes to taste (OPTIONAL)

--- Cheese Sauce with Butternut Squash

- 2 cans campbell's HEALTHY REQUEST condensed cheddar cheese soup. (2 cans = 2 cups condensed)
- 1 cup chicken broth
- 10 oz frozen butternut squash (or fresh)
- 3-1/2 tsp cornstarch + a little water to dissolve
- 1/4 tsp ground turmeric
- 1/2 tsp ground mustard
- 1/4 tsp cayenne pepper (OPTIONAL)
- 2 Tbsp reduced fat grated parmesan cheese topping
- 2 tsp "Kernel Seasons" nacho cheddar popcorn seasoning, or other brand cheese popcorn sprinkles
  - flavored popcorn seasonings can be found at your grocery store next to the popcorn

Serving Size:
Yields: 3qt. Casserole
Servings: 12
Serving Size: 2/3 cup

Points:
1 Serving = 3 points
2 Servings = 7 points
3 Servings = 10 points

--- Ricotta Parmesan Pasta Dumplings:

- 2 cups All Purpose Flour (or your preferred flour)
- 1 tsp baking powder
- 2 large eggs
- 1/2 cup Fat Free Ricotta Cheese
- 1 Tbsp reduced fat grated Parmesan cheese topping
- 1/2 tsp salt
- additional water to mix (around 1/4 cup)
- olive oil cooking spray
- **CAJONES.** No really,… you need to step out of your comfort zone big-time to make this, so buckle up buttercup!

--- The "Filling" ingredients:

You can completely customize this. The ingredients listed below are what I chose to use. Think of my filling as a base/guide for your own. However, volume is key.

- 1 LARGE onion, chopped
- 8 oz package mushrooms, sliced
- 2 medium garlic cloves, chopped
- 5 oz chopped tuscan kale. (color and crunch)
- 3/4 cup chicken broth, divided

Now… let the fun begin!

By fun, I mean you'll wish that booze was 0 points, and you'll probably want to hire a maid service to clean your kitchen when you're done.

Directions: *(hold on to your knickers)*

1. Mix all of the ingredients for the Italian Sausage together in a large bowl, to combine. Cook in a large pan, with cooking spray, over high heat. Break up the meat into small pieces. Remove from heat and set aside.

2. Spray the same pan with cooking spray and add the onions, garlic and 1/2 cup chicken broth. Cook uncovered for 4-5 minutes. Add sliced mushrooms and cook another 5 minutes until mushrooms are darkened and cooked through.

3. Add the chopped kale, italian sausage and an additional 1/4 cup chicken broth. Cover and cook on medium heat for 15 minutes, or until kale is soft, but still retains a slight crunch to the ribs. You don't want them TOO firm. When finished cooking, set aside.

4. Empty the bag of butternut squash into a steamer, then cover and steam for 15 minutes. If you don't have a steamer, you can put it in a gallon ziplock bag with a little water and microwave on high for 2-3 minutes. When finished cooking, set aside.

5. In a medium saucepot, heat the soup, chicken broth, dissolved cornstarch, turmeric, ground mustard and cheese flavored popcorn seasoning until heated through and thickened from the cornstarch.

6. Add the steamed butternut squash, Parmesan cheese and the cheese sauce mixture to a food processor and process until smooth. Return to the saucepot and heat again until the sauce thickens once again. Remove from heat and set aside.

Continued

7. In a large mixing bowl, or stand mixer combine the flour eggs, Ricotta, Parmesan, baking powder and salt. Start mixing the ingredients together, it WILL BE DRY! Gradually add water, a little at a time, it should take around 1/4 cup to form the ball. You want it to be a little on the drier side so that you don't have to add a lot of flour to it later.

8. Take your large 2 cup ricotta dough ball and cut it into 2 separate 1 cup sections. Then, cut each 1 cup section into 8 small sections, like pictured above.

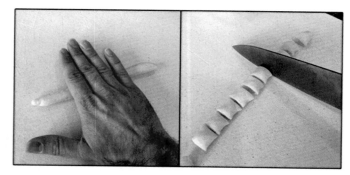

9. To avoid adding points from a lot of flour for dusting, we're going to lightly spritz a cutting board with cooking spray. Take each 1/8 section of pasta dough and use your palm to roll it out into long ropes, about as thick as your pinky finger. Don't worry, the gnocchi (yes, I'm calling them gnocchi dangit, it's my recipe! lol) will nearly double in size while cooking. After you slice the dough into gnocchi, lightly spray them with olive oil cooking spray and set them aside in a bowl. This will help them to not stick together, as well as add more flavor.

10. To make cooking easier, once you have a 1/2 cup of dough cut into gnocchi, drop them into a large pot of boiling water. These cook FAST. Allow the gnocchi to boil for 3-4 minutes. Scoop the dumplings into a strainer and immediately rinse them under cool water to stop them from cooking. I don't care if you pasta lovers are gasping in shock, do it. You've gone this far, just follow my lead, jelly bean. When you have rinsed that batch off, set it aside in a bowl and repeat the process until all of the pasta is finished.

11. In a laaaaaaaarge vessel of some type (I used a huge roasting pan, though you can use 2 large mixing bowls, combine the gnocchi with all of the filling and the cheese sauce. Gently fold together until all of the ingredients are mixed. Pour everything into a 13"x9" casserole dish that has been lightly sprayed with cooking spray.

12. Bake your cheesy gnocchi casserole in a 350 degree oven for 30-40 minutes, or until the sauce is bubbling around the edges and the casserole is warmed throughout. Remove from the oven and allow to sit for 15 minutes.

Spiced Cranberry Sauce

This is worlds removed from that canned goop you're used to

I tried my best to make as many low point side dishes as able this past Thanksgiving, but I naturally wasn't able to make everything that people requested. The most requested side that I couldn't get to was Cranberry Sauce. THANKFULLY, a wonderful friend from Connect, "@mugglemama2017" came to the rescue. She gave me permission to include her amazing Spiced Cranberry Sauce in this section.

Her cranberry sauce is a low point thing of beauty. It's sweet, tangy, has tremendous depth of flavor from the cinnamon, cloves, nutmeg, allspice, ginger and orange zest. Throw in a little bit of spiced rum and you won't even care about eating the main course, you'll be off, huddled in a corner with a bowl of this sauce and a spoon. You'll probably be clutching it like Gollum from The Lord of The Rings, calling it "Myyyy Preeeeecious" and snarling at passers-by.

Servings Info.:
Yield: 4 cups
Servings: 16
Serving Size: 1/4 cup

Point Values: **
1-3 serving = 0 points
4-11 servings = 1 point

NOTES:
- If you are unable to purchase **Sukrin Gold** brown sugar substitute, you can try using the following options instead:
  * **Real Brown Sugar:** 1/3 cup of real brown sugar will take this up to 1 point per 1/4 cup, which is great.
  * **SWERVE Brown Sugar:** Another 0 point brown sugar.
  * **Sugar Free Maple (pancake) Syrup**: Replace the 1/3 cup of Sukrin Gold with 1/4 cup of sugar free syrup.
  * **Root Beer:** Yep, sounds funky, but it's a viable option. Root beer has a complex caramel flavor and though it WILL change the flavor profile slightly, 1/4 cup of root beer is only 1 ingredient point.

- If you don't want to use spiced rum, you can either leave it out, or you can substitute it with 1 teaspoon of rum extract, which can be found in the spice aisle next to the vanilla extract.

Ingredients:
- 24 ounces fresh or frozen cranberries, divided
- 1 cup sweetener *(monkfruit, swerve, splenda, etc)*
- 3/4 cup water, divided
- 1/3 cup Sukrin Gold **
  (or other low point brown sugar alternative)
- 2 tablespoons orange juice
- Zest from 1 orange
- 2 teaspoons ground cinnamon
- 1/2 teaspoon ground allspice
- 1/2 teaspoon salt
- 1/2 teaspoon freshly grated nutmeg
- 1/8 teaspoon ground ginger
- 1/8 teaspoon ground cloves
- 1 tablespoon spiced rum *(optional)***

Directions:
1. Place half (12 oz) cranberries, monkfruit sweetener, 1/2 cup of water, brown sugar substitute, orange juice, orange zest, cinnamon, allspice, salt, nutmeg, ginger and cloves into a medium sauce pan and bring to a boil over medium-low to medium heat.
2. Cook, stirring occasionally until most berries start to pop, about 10 minutes. Add the other 12 oz. of cranberries, 1/4 cup water and cook for an additional 5-10 minutes or until most berries have popped.
3. Remove from heat, stir in spiced rum (if using), and let cool for 30 minutes. Adjust consistency with additional water, as needed.
4. Serve immediately or place in an airtight container and store in the refrigerator. Reheat prior to serving.

Reaching "Lifetime" on Sept. 22, 2018 with MuggleMama in Sacramento, CA

Acknowledgements

Hey, I can't name you all, but I came up with a nice cheat

There are so many people in Connect that I would like to thank, but c'mon folks, I'm following over 2,000 of you. There's no way I can mention each and every one of you that has impacted my journey since joining Weight Watchers. I DO however need to give a tremendous thank you to **@olahou** and **@69gabygirl** for spending weeks, on multiple occasions, fixing all of my errors. Only to have me put in new ones all over again thanks to my infamous late night revisions. How I didn't turn you two into raging alcoholics with my typos... I have no idea. Outside of this book I'd like to thank **@kimberly_grubbs** and **@daddybrat** for helping inspire me to finally start working out after I reached goal back in March. For those of you that don't follow them, you should.

I'd also like to thank the ladies out in Kentucky, especially **@kygoatgirl** and her WW studio folks. I swear that some day I'm going to make it to one of your meetings! Along those lines, **@mugglemama2017**, thank you. This past September she and her studio's leader invited me to speak at their meeting 7 hours north of where I live. I was given the floor, allowed to speak to everyone about how I prepare food to be lower in points and why I believe that it is so beneficial, answer questions, give tips and advice. It was an AMAZING moment of validation for me and my approach to cooking.

Then, of course there's my Connect "Sisters From Other Misters" crew. I can't name you all... because there are A LOT of you... a lot. There are so many of you ladies that have been so ridiculously encouraging, uplifting and supportive of me during this entire process. If you're reading this thinking "Golly, *Daniel's always really nice to me, I wonder if I'm a Sister From Another Mister?*" Then yes... yes you are!!!! That counts for you ladies that act like you're my volunteer marketing department. I always get a kick out of seeing the same couple of you tagging every single member in creation that posts they are new to WW, then telling them to follow me lol. A few notable mentions: *ktownkim, jfo_shizzle, mmkrizan, mfitch57, luckyclover1215, tiff89@aol.com, arroy0, faithisfat, jsmude, pyrophage, satlas, woodsy1955, carolray373, goldieloxpt, erinnrobertson, MARIARACHAEL12, leesha_jay, abbylandon0522, jjzcl12, trianarael, hellohealthyweight, dtspilde, FLYNNHE, kaylinejohnson, maggiez46, dodgermom59, snifferbiscuits, rosina8769, stina062762, javakidd1, back2me16, brittany77w, bsamsel427, CAKE.RIOT!!!! cherrir and the #UHCCL, cottontop78, darartist, dgibbs9, monkmom04, lisa2b50, awfoster0105, longhornsooner95, boombel, ncbluehog, dkhofheinz, emilybronte, krscully3, mannygano75, mecaara, justin.wallen79, mprospero, apostolic_lady, mgn426, zdlsh47, isabella_spilde* ... and, and, and.... THERE ARE TOO MANY OF YOU!!! How about this as a compromise?

Now, I know that you were probably worried that I would forget to mention you _____, but boy were wrong! You're awesome! You're the bee's knees! ... The cat's pajamas! 😬 😬   (insert your name here)

A few of the people who inspired me early on with their own recipes, which got the wheels turning in my head are: *silvy10131, chattykathyp* and *mlivinrn1*. There were a few more, but you 3 are the ones stuck in my mind. Lately, I've been loving going to look at the food pics from *mugglemama2017, mappleby777, diaryofawimpygirl, becca1007* and *hannahamil@aol.com*.

I also have to give an overwhelmingly heart felt thank you to **@andmatsmom**. I still remember when you tagged me in a message all those months ago, regarding the loss of your son and asking me to make that meal for your family. In the time since then, you have had a tremendous influence on me. You've offered suggestions for different meals and recipes I should make, given me tips for ways to improve my cooking... and you always offer your input with kindness and thoughtfulness. You've been a great encouragement and sounding-board for me to bounce ideas off of. Thank you for making me do the Thanksgiving recipes. Don't forget that I owe your husband a fresh pan of my 2 point Lasagna of awesomeness.

I'd also like to call out the big dog... **Mudhustler**. Thank you for your patience and repeated help with answering my questions and steering me in the right direction through some troubled waters recently. Thank you.

Onto the in-person people, this one's a lot easier. Thank you to my Wife, Dad, Brothers, Anngela and Mom. Thank you to Pastor Kevyn for making me see that THIS IS MY MINISTRY. Everyone at Valley Park Church, the Flores and Victorio families. Jay Levi and Julie Watts for pushing me to learn how to do graphic layout, which ultimately allowed me to design this entire publication on my own. Thank you everyone.

Closing Thoughts

The Musings of Baron von Hallakstein

Baron Daniel von Hallakstein VII, Lord of Gluttonia
Protector of Glutons and Slayer of Smart Points

As you've probably realized by now, this wasn't a regular cookbook, there's a great reason for that. This is a cookbook in-progress. Every single page that you've read (up to the holiday side dishes), is actually the first introductory section of a full sized, all encompassing cookbook that I am continuing to work on. This entire cooking guide is actually the first 2 sections of that book, the Introduction, followed by the Sauces. If you think that this first part was great, just wait until I start adding more sections onto it.

The final completed cookbook will, of course, include the contents of this guide, followed by sections for low point dips and dressings, appetizers and snacks, breakfasts, side dishes, entrees, and, best of all, desserts and baked goods.. It is going to be awesome.

If there is one thing that I would ask of you, it's that you PLEASE share with me your triumphs and setbacks in the kitchen. We're all stronger together and we're all walking the same path. If you use my Recipe Builder tutorial to tweak a recipe to be lower in points and you want to show that baby off? Post it in Connect! Use the hashtag *#RecipeBuilderChallenge*, along with what the original points per servings were, followed by what you lowered it to with ingredient swaps. After tweaking recipes a few times, through trial and error, you'll find techniques that really work for you. Share those in your post so they might help others. Need help with a recipe? Ask! Heck, feel free to submit a question to me directly through my website's contact form. It may take me a day or two to get back to you, but I will.

The reason why I chose to included recipes for sauces in this guide is because, for lack of a better way to put it, "Sauces will set you free!" How many times have you felt that you were getting bored of chicken, turkey, or fish? How many times have you told yourself that you are sick and tired of the same old vegetables? Well, now you have 30 sauces that are EXTREMELY LOW IN POINTS that you can toss on them to immediately kick them up 10 notches! Toss some broccoli with 1/4 cup of my cheese sauce for 1 point, or pour it on chips for lower point nachos. Instead of regular butter, dip lobster into my butter sauce for 0 points. If nothing else, these 30 sauces give you tons of options for jazzing up a boring dish.

Along with the continued expansion of the cookbook, I'll also be launching a FREE Community Recipe Sharing website. This will allow all of us to be able to upload/post, search, comment on and rate each others recipes, all in one place, without having to scour pinterest and instagram for recipes. That will be happening soon and I'm extremely excited about it! There's a LOT of great stuff that's just over the horizon for all of us.

WE'VE GOT THIS!!!!